AYN RAND AND THE RUSSIAN
INTELLIGENTSIA

Marina Mogilner, Associate Professor, University of Illinois at Chicago, USA

Willard Sunderland, Henry R. Winkler Professor of Modern History, University of Cincinnati, USA

PUBLISHED TITLES

Pussy Riot: Speaking Punk to Power, Eliot Borenstein

Memory Politics and the Russian Civil War: Reds Versus Whites, Marlene Laruelle and Margarita Karnysheva

Russian Utopia: A Century of Revolutionary Possibilities, Mark Steinberg

Racism in Modern Russia, Eugene M. Avrutin

Meanwhile, In Russia: Russian Memes and Viral Video Culture, Eliot Borenstein

Ayn Rand and the Russian Intelligentsia: The Origins of an Icon of the American Right, Derek Offord

UPCOMING TITLES

Art, History and the Making of Russian National Identity: Vasily Surikov, Viktor Vasnetsov, and the Remaking of the Past, Stephen M. Norris

Russia and the Jewish Question: A Modern History, Robert Weinberg

The Soviet Gulag: History and Memory, Jeffrey S. Hardy

The Afterlife of the 'Soviet Man': Rethinking Homo Sovieticus, Gulnaz Sharafutdinova

The Multiethnic Soviet Union and Its Demise, Brigid O'Keeffe

Russian Food since 1800: Empire at Table, Catriona Kelly

A Social History of the Russian Army, Roger R. Reese

Why We Need Russian Literature, Angela Brintlinger

Nuclear Russia, Paul Josephson

AYN RAND AND THE RUSSIAN INTELLIGENTSIA

THE ORIGINS OF AN ICON OF THE AMERICAN RIGHT

Derek Offord

BLOOMSBURY ACADEMIC
LONDON • NEW YORK • OXFORD • NEW DELHI • SYDNEY

BLOOMSBURY ACADEMIC
Bloomsbury Publishing Plc
50 Bedford Square, London, WC1B 3DP, UK
1385 Broadway, New York, NY 10018, USA
29 Earlsfort Terrace, Dublin 2, Ireland

BLOOMSBURY, BLOOMSBURY ACADEMIC and the Diana logo are
trademarks of Bloomsbury Publishing Plc

First published in Great Britain 2022

Series design by Tjaša Krivec
Cover image: Writer Ayn Rand testifies before the House Un-American
Activities Committee on October 20, 1947. (© Bettmann / Getty Images)

A catalogue record for this book is available from the British Library.

A catalog record for this book is available from the Library of Congress.

ISBN: PB: 978-1-3502-8394-7
         HB: 978-1-3502-8395-4
         ePDF: 978-1-3502-8396-1
         eBook: 978-1-3502-8393-0

Typeset by Integra Software Services Pvt. Ltd.
Printed and bound in Great Britain

To find out more about our authors and books visit www.bloomsbury.com
and sign up for our newsletters.

To Dorinda, Catherine and Helen

CONTENTS

Acknowledgements   xi
A Note on the Text   xii

Introduction   1

1   Ayn Rand and her Russian background   9
Upbringing, education and personality   9
Russia's Jewish minority   12
Russian culture in the twilight of the old regime   16
Intellectual and literary influences   20

2   Rand and the Russian intellectual tradition   27
The Russian intelligentsia and its outlook   27
The intelligentsia's way of thinking and writing   32
The novel as a vehicle for philosophical polemic   36

3   Rand and Russian literary models   41
Rand as a dystopian novelist   41
Rand as a revolutionary novelist   48
Rand and the Socialist Realist novel   56

4   Ethical, metaphysical and epistemological questions   61
Altruism is bad and egoism is good   61
Ordinary and extraordinary members of the human race   65
Dualism and monism, determinism, reason and volition   70

Contents

5   Politics and economics   75

    An anarchist's utopia?   75

    The exclusivity of Rand's New Jerusalem   79

    Democracy and economic distribution in Rand's
    ideal world   83

6   Geopolitics   87

    Russia and Europe in Russian thought   87

    A war of the worlds   90

    Making America great again   92

Conclusion   99

Notes   103
Selected bibliography   115
Index   119

ACKNOWLEDGEMENTS

I am grateful to the seven anonymous scholars who have reviewed the manuscript of this book at some stage of its development. Many of their comments have helped to broaden and improve the work and shape its final version. I also warmly thank the editors of the Russian Shorts series, Eugene Avrutin and Stephen Norris, for their own useful guidance, and Rhodri Mogford, Bloomsbury's commissioning editor, for his advice and role in steering me towards completion of the book. I am indebted too to Anthony Grenville, who works in different fields to my own, for his reading of my manuscript and advice on one section of it in particular. Most of all, I thank Dorinda, my wife, for her own patient reading of the manuscript and her insights and numerous suggestions. I am of course solely responsible myself for any flaws which may remain in spite of the best efforts of all these readers.

Bristol
October 2021

A NOTE ON THE TEXT

Transliteration and spelling of Russian names

I have followed the Library of Congress (LoC) system of transliteration in my text and notes, with some exceptions. Russian surnames ending in -ский have been rendered with the commonly used form -sky, which is more familiar than -skii to the non-specialist anglophone reader. The anglicized form Herzen is preferred to the transliterated form of the surname of this thinker, Gertsen. I have also used the common English forms of the surnames of the novelists Gorky and Lev Tolstoy, the poet Mayakovsky, and the composers Rachmaninov and Scriabin. For Russian forenames, transliterated forms (Aleksandr, Petr and so forth) have been used, except for the names of monarchs (Alexander, Catherine, Nicholas, Peter), which are translated, and in the cases of Alexander Herzen and Alexander Pushkin, both of whom are more often referred to in this way in English texts.

Dates

From 1700 until February 1918, the calendar used in Russia was the Julian calendar, which was behind the Gregorian calendar used in the West by eleven days in the eighteenth century, twelve in the nineteenth and thirteen in the twentieth. Dates given in this book are in the Old Style (OS, i.e. according to the Julian calendar) when they relate to things that happened in Russia before the Bolsheviks' introduction of the New (i.e. Gregorian) Style (NS).

References in the text

All references in the text to *AS*, *F* and *WL* are to the editions of *Atlas Shrugged*, *The Fountainhead* and *We the Living* cited in the selected bibliography.

INTRODUCTION

In *The Fountainhead* (1943) and *Atlas Shrugged* (1957), the two novels for which she is chiefly remembered, the prose writer and self-styled Objectivist philosopher known by her pen name Ayn Rand articulated ideas about society, politics, economics and the goals of human life that have had wide and lasting appeal in the United States and in certain quarters beyond it. Her fiction has been praised by generations of conservatives from the New York intellectual Right of the 1950s and Reaganites of the 1980s to members of the Tea Party in the 2010s. Donald Trump sees Howard Roark, the hero of *The Fountainhead*, as a role model.[1] Alan Greenspan, chairman of the Board of Governors of the US Federal Reserve from 1987 to 2006, was a disciple and member of Rand's entourage, or 'Collective' as it was ironically and affectionately known, from the mid-1950s.[2] Other prominent politicians and public figures who are said to have been attracted to Rand's ideas include Rex Tillerson, a former chief executive of ExxonMobil and Trump's secretary of state for a little over a year, his successor as secretary of state Mike Pompeo, and Andrew Puzder, a lawyer, businessman and briefly Trump's nominee for the post of secretary of labour.[3] Paul Ryan, the former Republican speaker of the House of Representatives, has said that it was the influence of Rand that made him enter politics.[4] Rand's writings, which the fast-food chain Burger King once advised its executives to read,[5] have also by now become widespread cultural reference points among wealthy bankers, CEOs, tech moguls and major figures in Silicon Valley, as well as right-wing politicians.[6] In the UK, her admirers include Daniel Hannan, an author, columnist, former Conservative member of the European Parliament and leading advocate of Britain's exit from the European Union, and Sajid Javid, a former Conservative home secretary and chancellor of the exchequer and current secretary of state for health and social care, who claims to re-read *The Fountainhead* frequently, especially Roark's climactic court-room oration.[7]

According to the official website of the Ayn Rand Institute (ARI), an organization set up in 1985 to propagate Rand's ideas after her death in 1982, Rand's books have sold over 37 million copies, including some 9 million copies of *The Fountainhead* and 10 million of *Atlas Shrugged*.[8] However, it is not a straightforward matter to explain this commercial success, since Rand's answers to the moral questions that she placed at the centre of her outlook and their political corollaries provoke a highly negative response in many readers. It is therefore useful to recognize that different readerships are applying widely differing criteria when they form their judgements. These criteria range from assumed standards of literary excellence or philosophical rigour, notions about the proper balance between the individual and society, respect for or aversion to free-market economics, and political orientation to satisfaction or dissatisfaction with the explanations Rand offers of the goals of human life and with her definitions of personal fulfilment.

As far as literary assessment is concerned, Rand's novels have features that we associate with the sort of popular fiction one expects to find in an airport departure lounge. They are long but sometimes pacey page-turners with a large cast of characters, several plot lines, intrigue, some suspense and occasional violence. These features should not be seen as flaws in themselves; after all, they account to some extent for the readability of Honoré de Balzac, Charles Dickens or Fedor Dostoevsky. On the other hand, Rand's narratives are also interrupted by self-righteous ideological orations which it is unlikely many readers peruse conscientiously, such as the monologue some seventy pages long that is delivered to the American nation in a radio broadcast by her paragon of men, John Galt, in *Atlas Shrugged*. Her characters are either mouthpieces for her own views or caricatures of types of person she deplores. Their speech is leaden and implausible. As for plot, which Rand considered '*the* crucial attribute of a novel',[9] it may be melodramatic or take a ludicrous turn, as when another of the heroes of *Atlas Shrugged*, Ragnar Danneskjöld, who is a Norwegian pirate [*sic*], has his ship raze American steel plants to the ground with long-range naval guns (*AS*: 570). Rand also lacked the human empathy that the accomplished novelist surely needs in addition to powers of observation and rational understanding. It is consequently unsurprising that 'the nearly universal consensus among literary critics', in the opinion of Jennifer Burns, one of Rand's principal biographers, is that Rand 'is a bad writer'.[10]

If, on the other hand, we look for reasons why Rand's fiction has had such appeal to readers beyond the critical literary world, then it is surely on its didactic, exhortatory and ideological content that we should focus. For many readers, Rand's writings offer a form of revelation. They provide guidance of a quasi-philosophical nature on how people should live their lives, make decisions, conduct relationships and fulfil their human potential. Numerous admirers from many backgrounds and walks of life have recorded their feeling that her work has in some way liberated, empowered, inspired or vindicated them and increased their confidence in the validity of their own experience and ambitions.[11] On another level, Rand's corpus amounts to an exploration of American identity. For this reason, it has been suggested, 'a brief infatuation with Rand' has become a 'common American adolescent rite of passage'.[12] For a right-leaning adult readership, meanwhile, Rand's merit lies in her defence of capitalism and her belief that, in Jonathan Chait's words, 'the natural market distribution of income is inherently moral, and [that] the central struggle of politics is to free the successful from having the fruits of their superiority redistributed' by envious parasites or humanitarians with a social conscience.[13] Or as Burns puts it, Rand's writings have functioned as 'the ultimate gateway drug to life on the right'.[14] It is understandable, then, that Rand's reception has been much more favourable in the business world than in the literary world.[15] Moreover, the erotic aspect of her novels, which contain explicit descriptions of (often violent) sex that were unusual in mid-twentieth-century fiction, no doubt helps, for some readers, to glamourize the arrogant and acquisitive ideologues whom she heroizes.

It is not necessary to subscribe to a traditionalist view that only canonical literary works warrant lasting attention in order to agree that Rand's writings deserve close study. Irrespective of the reader's opinion of their intrinsic intellectual or literary quality, they have extrinsic value of various kinds. It cannot be denied, for example, that they remain intensely topical, as attested by the introductory list of influential admirers I have given, or that they are a conspicuous feature of the context of which historians of early-twenty-first-century Western culture and politics must take account. As Lisa Duggan has argued, it may be difficult for readers who are not drawn into the Randian cult to refrain from explaining her work 'as the compensatory fantasy life of a tortured soul who was perhaps a sociopath'. Nonetheless, Duggan insists, we must engage with this work in order to understand Rand's great impact on the world fashioned by the rise of neoliberalism.[16] Above all, Rand's work is instructive as an example of exploration of the limits to which one might dare to apply unconventional ideas in practice, as a quintessential expression of an ideological paradigm and way of thinking, and as a vivid account of the possible implications of living in accordance with certain values.

*

Both Rand's major novels squarely address the social, political, cultural and intellectual realities of contemporary American life from the 1930s to the mid-1950s, albeit with certain striking omissions, such as the Second World War and race relations. The mid-twentieth century was a period when the United States was becoming an industrial and military superpower and when federal government required greater financial resources to fund not only the expansion and equipment of the armed forces and the infrastructure befitting a global power but also social programmes which were coming to be regarded as necessary for the public good. During what was perceived by the American Right as the Red Decade, the extended reach of the state and its imposition of taxation for this latter purpose, broadly conceived, were exemplified by the New Deal implemented by Franklin D. Roosevelt between 1933 and 1936 in response to the Great Depression the United States had undergone after the Wall Street Crash of 1929. Centrally coordinated and costly national effort would also be essential, of course, during the Second World War and for post-war reconstruction, both at home and abroad. At the same time, laissez-faire economic policy was being challenged, in the United States and Europe, by economists such as John Maynard Keynes who advocated government action to stimulate sluggish economies through state-funded projects without undue concern about creating deficits.[17] Rand is strongly opposed to these extensions of the role of the state and to elevation of the importance of collective interests at the perceived expense of the individual. Her opposition is already plainly felt in *The Fountainhead*, and in *Atlas Shrugged* it is unrestrained. Her stance has fresh appeal, moreover, in the current populist age, when trust in politicians, deference towards establishments and 'experts', respect for large bureaucratic and seemingly impersonal institutions, and a sense of belonging to an organic community have to a considerable extent broken down in advanced Western societies.

Rand's two major novels are located in twentieth-century America (though before the invention of the jet engine had transformed air travel, it seems!) and they articulate an aggressive, libertarian, anti-socialist form of American patriotism, but the observations they contain on America's condition and futurity are those of an outsider. Rand was an immigrant from revolutionary Russia who arrived in the United States, already intending to make it her permanent home, in February 1926, a few weeks after her twenty-first birthday. After taking advantage, rather ungratefully, of the hospitality of members of her extended Jewish family who had settled in Chicago, she travelled to California, where she obtained work in Hollywood, in the first instance as an extra and then as a junior script writer in the studios of Cecil B. DeMille. There she met Frank O'Connor, whom she married in 1929 and who remained loyal and supportive despite her fourteen-year adulterous relationship, which began in 1954, with a Canadian acolyte twenty-five years her junior, Nathan Blumenthal, or Nathaniel Branden, as he renamed himself when he fell under her spell. She continued to live in the United States until her death, of lung cancer, at the age of seventy-seven.

The young Rand arrived in the United States armed, as we shall see, with undoubted intelligence and determination, a broad education of high quality, an ambition to become a writer and a keen sense of her personal superiority. She also harboured deep cultural, political and economic resentments against her country of origin. She would make a point of repudiating the altruistic idealism and strong sense of civic duty that typified members of the intelligentsia that had come to play such a decisive role in Russian life by the time Rand was born. In defiance of them, she would produce an apologia for a different kind of moral and intellectual elite and would mount a brutal defence of self-interested individualism and unregulated capitalism. It is these aspects of Rand's novels that account, at bottom, for the lasting appeal and influence they have enjoyed in certain conservative and neoliberal circles in the Western anglophone world and for their continuing topicality in the twenty-first century. At the same time, she brought with her to America a burning interest in certain philosophical questions and literary themes that had long animated the Russian intelligentsia, notions of literary types that Russian writers had explored, familiarity with the Russian novel and sub-genres of it and a conception shared by many Russian writers of the uses to which prose fiction should be put. Central to this Russian legacy were certain intellectual traits and writing habits characteristic of the *intelligent* or *intelligentka*, as the male and female members of the Russian intelligentsia were respectively known. These included the polemical edge, the angry tone, the black-and-white colouring of her opinions and the polarized style of thinking that would be so striking in Rand's fiction. Her ideas themselves were informed by debates in late-nineteenth- and early-twentieth-century Russian thought and literature. In short, Rand was in many ways a descendant of the Russian intelligentsia, particularly its radical wing.

*

In support of my claim about Rand's relationship to the pre-revolutionary Russian intelligentsia and literary community, the first three chapters of this book will establish the various contexts in which Rand was formed. Chapter 1 provides biographical information and a sketch of the Russian Silver Age in which she was brought up. Chapter 2 considers the nature of the Russian intelligentsia, the questions it tended to address and the modes of thinking and writing to which Rand had become accustomed in her native land before she emigrated. Chapter 3 examines some of the varieties of the novel of ideas with which Rand's prose fiction has affinities and which contain ideas and use techniques that help her to expose what she regards as dangerous faults in contemporary American society and to suggest ways of eliminating them.

The three chapters that make up the second half of the book look more closely at the ways in which Rand used prose fiction to popularize the quasi-philosophical outlook she constructed within the Russian intellectual framework she knew. For Rand, as for large swathes of the Russian intelligentsia and literary community, the key to the transformations of the world that she hoped to bring about lay in ethics as much as in politics.[18] My account of her ideas therefore begins, in Chapter 4, with her definition of the good, which inverts conventional valuations of altruism and egoism. This chapter also briefly explores her views on metaphysical and epistemological matters, such as the presence or absence of a spiritual dimension in human beings, the extent to which human actions are determined by factors humans cannot control, the role of reason in human conduct and the capacity of humans to exercise free will. In Chapter 5, we turn to the political philosophy Rand intends her ethics and metaphysics to underpin. The utopia she imagines is designed to enable humans of the kind she heroizes to find full self-realization. In sketching it, Rand necessarily touches upon such subjects as the distribution of what a society produces, the regulation or deregulation of economic activity and levels of taxation. She is much less interested, though, in the institution of majoritarian democracy on which American political life rests. In Chapter 6, finally, Rand's outlook is placed in the geopolitical arena, which had fascinated Russian thinkers and writers as they identified themselves as internationalists or nationalists and speculated about what some nowadays call the 'clash of civilizations'.[19] Aware of the contributions of late imperial Russian intellectuals to thinking about the distinctive character and historical mission of particular peoples, Rand developed her own conception of 'Americanism'. In sum, all facets of the outlook that crystallizes in her major fiction are coloured by the intellectual and literary legacy that she brought with her from Russia to the United States. There is every reason to agree with one of her most authoritative biographers, Anne Heller, when she observes that although Rand never returned to Russia after her departure from it in 1926, in many ways she never really left it.[20]

Rand left a substantial body of writings, both fictional and non-fictional.[21] Of the two novels for which she is chiefly remembered, *Atlas Shrugged* is by some way the more important. Rand's technique, the character types she creates and the broad contours of her outlook are all in evidence in *The Fountainhead*, to be sure.[22] In that novel, she already rejects the notion of the 'social good',[23] opposes the use of taxation for federal projects and expresses her dislike of socialism of every complexion, from communism to social democracy. Nonetheless, her 'philosophy' was not yet fully developed by the time she finished *The Fountainhead*. As she told her readers in 1957, that novel was 'only an overture' to the even longer work she had by then completed (*AS*: [1071, unpaginated]). It is in *Atlas Shrugged*, therefore, that we find the most comprehensive and definitive expression of Rand's belief that superior humans – the only humans she cared about – could fully realize themselves by living for no-one but themselves in an unregulated free market.

CHAPTER 1
AYN RAND AND HER RUSSIAN BACKGROUND

Upbringing, education and personality

Née Alisa Zinov'evna Rosenbaum, Rand was the eldest of three daughters of upwardly mobile Jewish parents living in St Petersburg, the capital of the Russian Empire. She was born on 20 January 1905, eleven days after Bloody Sunday, the day when the Russian imperial guard killed many unarmed demonstrators marching to the Winter Palace – an event that helped to precipitate the first Russian Revolution. She was brought up in the intense intellectual atmosphere of this most cosmopolitan of Russia's cities (renamed Petrograd in 1914) during the last years of the old autocratic regime.

The city in which Rand grew up and was educated was Russia's 'window on to Europe' (the phrase belongs originally to an eighteenth-century Italian traveller, Francesco Algarotti). In a passage written with a literary polish that is rare in her writings, Rand herself described the awe-inspiring nature of this historic city in her first published novel, *We the Living* (1936). St Petersburg had virtues which readers of her fiction will recognize as quintessentially Randian. It was 'a monument to the spirit of man', having been founded 'against the will of nature' by Peter the Great (sole ruler 1696–1725) on an inhospitable swamp. It was 'the work of man who knows what he wants'. It did not need a soul, for it had a mind. In the language of the Russians, Rand pointed out, it had always been 'he', unlike female-gendered Moscow (*WL*: 224, 226).

Life in an aspirational family resident in this metropolis introduced Rand from her earliest years to a Europeanized cultural world, including its literature (Victor Hugo was an early favourite), in which she took a precocious interest. She received private tuition in French and German. Her imagination was also stimulated, in the summer of 1914, by a European tour of the sort prized by educated Russians, in the course of which the family visited Vienna, Switzerland, Paris and London, where, Rand would claim, she resolved at the age of nine to become a writer. Having returned to Russia in August 1914, by which time the country was at war, Rand entered a highly respected girl's *gimnaziia*, or high school, directed by Mariia Stoiunina, the widow of a distinguished pedagogue and a school friend of Anna Snitkina, who in 1867 had become the second wife of Dostoevsky.[1] Here Alisa benefitted from a broad education in the humanities and sciences. Contemporaries at the school included Ol'ga Nabokova, younger sister of the future novelist Vladimir Nabokov.[2]

Alisa was only in the early stages of her schooling in the *gimnaziia* when the two revolutions of 1917 broke out: first, the February Revolution, which resulted in the collapse of tsarism and the establishment of the provisional government headed from July that year by Aleksandr Kerensky, whom the twelve-year-old Rand briefly worshipped, and then the October Revolution, in which the Bolsheviks, led by Lenin, seized power and began to govern by decree. In the late summer of 1918, after the outbreak of the post-revolutionary Civil War (1918–22), the Rosenbaum family fled to the Crimea, which initially supported the White side in this conflict, but three years later, after the Crimea too had fallen to the Bolsheviks, the family returned to Petrograd. At this point, Rand entered what had become the city's State University.[3] There she studied history and philosophy, before graduating in 1924.

For all her appetite for intellectual and cultural enrichment, Alisa was evidently a lonely and unhappy child. She was self-contained and liable both to cause offence to and to be easily disappointed by those whom she considered inferior, that is to say everybody who did not measure up to her ideals or childhood literary models.[4] One of her principal biographers plausibly speculates that 'the universe of moral principles' that Rand constructed in her twenties was built largely on some of her unhappy childhood experiences, including the difficulty she had in making friendships with her peers or winning approval. It also seems obvious that she had a troubled relationship with her mother.[5] Certainly, in her literary universe, from her first novel *We the Living* to *Atlas Shrugged*, mothers take the lead in criticizing their gifted children for their egotism, arrogance and obstinacy, to the bewilderment and resentment of these children themselves (*WL*: 25, 27, 257; *AS*: 37).

Every biographical account of her childhood and adolescence suggests that Rand also exhibited from an early age the self-absorption and lack of warmth towards others that characterize the heroes of her fiction, and these traits persisted throughout her adult life. As both human individual and author, she seems not to have experienced the emotions and affections which tend to bring humans together and inspire them with a sense of belonging to something larger than themselves. This absence of feeling is all of a piece with the obduracy of her characters and with their overwhelming prioritization of self over others and of rationality over compassion. We cannot but surmise that her extreme antipathy to socialism and her intense denigration of the altruism on which socialists may claim to base their political philosophy stem not merely from reasoning and from her personal experience of living under the emerging Bolshevik dictatorship but also from unfamiliarity with the pleasure that may be afforded to humans by companionship and social cooperation. Mentally rigid, she was unable to tolerate opinions different from her own and was arrogantly dismissive of those who disagreed with her. Intellect, according to her biographer Barbara Branden, was the ruling element of Rand's personality and the criterion by which she judged the worthiness of others. No quality of character that indicates considerate treatment of other people, such as generosity or kindness, ever elicited Rand's admiration. Emotions, to her mind, were merely the product of the thinking that a person had done or refused to do. Nor could she believe that humour was an important human characteristic, and she was contemptuous of the belief that one ought to be able to laugh at oneself.[6]

Even in the closest relationships formed in adulthood, moreover, Rand seems not so much to be bonding with fellow humans on an equal basis as creating forms of dependency, seeking to dominate her husband, friends, protégés and disciples. While bitterly opposed to totalitarianism on the ideological level, she surrounded herself in her sealed, censorious Collective with close-knit followers of whom she required absolute agreement and allegiance.[7] As Barbara Branden was astute enough to recognize in her biography, it suited Rand that these followers were so much younger than her and were 'still in the process of being formed'. Whether she was conscious of it or not, Rand 'was a woman with a powerful need for control', and the vulnerability of her young acolytes 'made possible an intellectual and moral dominance less likely to occur with accomplished men and women of her own age'. In this setting, over which she would preside like a renowned *salonnière*, Rand displayed a taste for sessions that resembled show trials, often led on her behalf by Nathaniel, in which cowed victims were subjected to psychiatric analysis and forced to confess to egregious breaches of the Randian moral and intellectual code.[8]

Russia's Jewish minority

Rand was not only an outsider temperamentally. As a member of a Jewish family, she also belonged to an ethnic minority of the Russian Empire which, viewed as a whole, endured much prejudice and persecution. Most members of this minority, which numbered almost 5 million by the time of the census of 1897, were confined to the so-called Pale of Settlement that had been created by Catherine II (Catherine the Great) in 1791. The Pale came to include the whole of Russian Poland, Lithuania, Belorussia, most of the Ukraine, the Crimea and Bessarabia. Prejudice against Jews was encouraged by the Orthodox Church and shared to some extent by the last two tsars, Alexander III (reigned 1881–94) and Nicholas II (1894–1917). Many prominent public figures, such as the publisher and long-time owner of the popular daily paper *New Times*, Aleksei Suvorin, and the renowned chemist Dmitrii Mendeleev, were notoriously anti-Semitic.[9] Dostoevsky's letters, notebooks and *Diary of a Writer* (1876–81) also expose a crude, hostile stereotyping of Jews.[10] In the reactionary climate of the 1880s, the opportunities available to Jews to improve their lot were limited by the imposition of quotas on the numbers of them who were permitted to enter secondary and higher education institutions, and such restrictions remained in force until the old regime collapsed in 1917. Over the same period, restrictions were also placed on the right of Jews to enter the legal profession, one of the most important institutions in Russia's embryonic civil society, in which Jews had achieved qualitative and quantitative prominence after the judicial reform of 1864 and the creation of a bar in 1866.[11]

The strong current of anti-Semitism in late imperial society and the Russian sense of being threatened by Jewish success in education and the emerging professions helped to license mob violence against Jewish communities. Pogroms, as episodes of such violence were known, had broken out in the south of Russia in the early 1880s after revolutionary terrorists of the People's Will party had assassinated Alexander II in March 1881, although Jews were not numerous or prominent in the People's Will in this period of its history. This early wave of racial violence ebbed when the unscrupulous nationalist Count Nikolai Ignat'ev was replaced as minister of the interior in 1882, but it swelled again in the years before, during and after the revolution of 1905. The Union of the Russian People, one of the new political parties that sprang up in 1905, appealed to anti-Semitic sentiment in the southern towns in the Pale and drew support from landlords, rich peasants (*kulaks*), bureaucrats, petty officials, the police and the Orthodox clergy. From 1906 to around the end of the decade, armed bands known as 'Black Hundreds' (*chernosotentsy*), emboldened by this proto-fascist organization, repeatedly attacked Jewish property. There were also mass expulsions of Jews from Russia's western borderlands during the First World War.

Given this climate of persecution, it is unsurprising that in due course many Jews did become active participants in the revolutionary movement. The Bund, a Jewish labour organization, played an important role in the development of the Russian Social-Democratic Labour Party (RSDLP), which was founded in 1898 in Minsk, one of the cities in the Pale. The man known by the revolutionary pseudonym Martov, who led the Mensheviks, one of the factions into which the RSDLP split in 1903, was a Jew, Iulii Tsederbaum. So were four of the seven members of the first Bolshevik politburo founded in 1917, including Lev Kamenev (Leo Rosenfeld), Leon Trotsky (Lev Bronstein) and Grigorii Zinov'iev (Hirsch Apfelbaum).

Although Russian anti-Semitism, and especially the pogroms, no doubt drove many Russian Jews either to enter revolutionary organizations or to emigrate, numerous others had been more or less successfully assimilated into Russian society outside the Pale of Settlement during the second half of the nineteenth century. Late imperial Russian Jewry, far from being a uniform community, was internally divided and fractious. Indeed, by the 1880s, it has been argued, there were in effect two Russian Jewries: on the one hand, the legally and culturally segregated Jews of the Pale and, on the other, those who were permitted – or had otherwise contrived – to live beyond the Pale and were striving for civic emancipation and social integration to the mutual advantage of both the late imperial state and themselves. For integrationists, acquisition of Russian culture was compatible with faithfulness to Jewish national culture, especially in private life. Such Jews might even view Russian identity as transnational and adoption of it as a means of participating in civic life.[12] In that respect, they would find themselves at odds with Zionists and Jewish socialists, not least because their limited and pragmatic attempts to secure gradual improvements in the condition of their ethnic group contrasted sharply with the grand narratives of Zionists, who craved their own homeland, and socialists, who dreamed of an egalitarian society in which all ethnic groups would be treated in the same way.

The Jewish bankers and stock-market speculators who flourished towards the end of the nineteenth century during Russia's late encounter with capitalist institutions, merchants, graduates seeking careers in the professions – all these groups were attracted to St Petersburg, both because of the commercial opportunities the city offered and because it was the centre of the empire's cultural life.[13] By the 1870s, St Petersburg had replaced Odessa as the headquarters of the empire's emerging Russian-Jewish culture and its Jews came to regard themselves, in a way that could be perceived as imperious, as leaders of Russian Jewry as a whole.[14] It was in this cosmopolitan milieu, where Jews were not so routinely subject to the privations, injustices and abuse suffered by the inhabitants of a shtetl in the Pale of Settlement, that Rand grew up. Barbara Branden is no doubt right to suppose that it is inconceivable that Rand never encountered anti-Semitism in St Petersburg. She is also justified in speculating that Rand may have omitted to mention such encounters because she habitually repressed memories of painful experience.[15] All the same, the Rosenbaums would seem to have led a comparatively secure and comfortable existence during Rand's childhood. Alisa's father was a pharmacist and her mother had trained as a dental practitioner, and as affluent professionals the Rosenbaums had spacious accommodation in the city's historic centre and employed a maid, a cook and a Belgian governess. Rand's sociable and socially ambitious mother arranged parties attended by professional people such as lawyers and doctors. The family may also have been partly protected from any of the consequences of anti-Semitism by uncles who continued the family tradition of making boots for the imperial army.[16]

As Jews who had undergone a secular education and were relatively well integrated into Russian society, Rand's parents evidently did not try strictly to inculcate Jewish practices in their children. Religion and religious observance, according to the account of her childhood that Rand gave to Branden, 'had little meaning or place' in the Rosenbaum household. The family observed Jewish holy days only in a perfunctory way and for a while. As for Rand herself, she would say in later years that the fact that she was born Jewish had no significance for her and that she had no emotional tie or sense of identification with Jews, or things Jewish.[17] The importance that the relatives who accommodated her in Chicago just after she had arrived in the United States attached to living as Jews and to attendance at their synagogue was therefore incomprehensible to their difficult guest from Russia. Rand's apparent lack of affinity with her ethnic community in the diaspora was of a piece with her general indifference to family bonds and loyalties and her dislike, in childhood and adolescence, of attachment to the particular family into which she happened to have been born.[18] On the philosophical level, Rand was pleased when others understood that her ethical views ran counter to 'the entire tradition of Judaeo-Christian ethics'.[19] If being Jewish left any trace in Rand's writings, then perhaps it was more because it seemed to this self-absorbed woman a condition to rebel against, like Russianness or belonging to a family, than because it offered certain respected traditions and values.

The Rosenbaums may not have been much troubled by anti-Semitism in pre-revolutionary Petrograd, but in the post-revolutionary Soviet Union a new disadvantage confronted them. As members of a commercial and property-owning middle class, the family represented the class enemy when viewed from the vantage point of revolutionary socialists. To the Bolsheviks, they were bourgeois shopkeepers whose property should now be expropriated by the supposedly proletarian state that had just come into being. Shortly after the October Revolution, when Alisa was twelve, the family's pharmacy business in Petrograd was duly closed by armed members of the party[20] – a misfortune that no doubt contributed to Rand's loathing of socialism.

Russian culture in the twilight of the old regime

In the closing decades of the nineteenth century, the Russian intelligentsia had begun to lose hope of softening the empire's autocratic government and radically improving the lives of Russia's people in the foreseeable future. Former idealists resigned themselves to 'small deeds', modest attempts to bring about gradual progress, and succumbed to that mood of futility that is felt so strongly in the turn-of-the-century stories and plays of Anton Chekhov. The first decade of Rand's life, on the other hand, was a silver age of Russian culture which bore comparison with the nineteenth-century golden age that ended with the deaths of Dostoevsky in 1881 and the novelist Ivan Turgenev in 1883 and with the transition of Lev Tolstoy around that time from masterly novelist to sage, moralist and pacifist anarchist. Living in St Petersburg, Rand was well-placed to appreciate this last intellectual and artistic flowering of imperial Russia, a cultural renaissance which seemed the more dazzling for the gloom that had preceded it.

New prose writers filled the void left by the deaths of the major classical authors, most notably Maksim Gorky, who would become a literary authority after the Bolsheviks came to power, and Ivan Bunin, who emigrated to France in 1920 and won the Nobel Prize for his prose fiction in 1933. However, it was chiefly in poetry and other art forms that the early-twentieth-century Russian cultural revival made itself felt. Aesthetic sensibility was prized at the expense of the social and political commitment in art on which the radical intelligentsia had insisted since the mid-nineteenth century. In literature, the rejection of realism and naturalism found expression, from around the turn of the century, in Symbolism, a movement of French and Belgian origin. The Russian Symbolists, such as Valerii Briusov, Viacheslav Ivanov and the outstanding poet among them, Aleksandr Blok, were highly cultured men who raised both the level of poetic craftsmanship and knowledge of foreign literature (many of them were translators as well as creative writers). They put forward a mystical view of the world as containing 'forests of symbols', valuing words as much for their sounds and associations as for their semantic meaning. Symbolists also expressed themselves in memorable novels, of which the most notable examples were Fedor Sologub's *Little Demon* (1908) and Andrei Belyi's *Silver Dove* (1909) and *Petersburg* (1913), both of which concern the philosophy of Russian history and explore the tension in it between its western and its eastern gaze.[21] The Symbolist movement began to lose momentum in the second decade of the twentieth century, but poetry continued to flourish and new movements proliferated, especially Acmeism, whose main representative was Nikolai Gumilev, and Futurism, which was founded by Velemir Khlebnikov but is chiefly associated with Vladimir Mayakovsky, who came to be seen as the poet of the October Revolution.

The new aestheticism informed other branches of art, besides poetry and some prose fiction. It was manifested, for example, in art criticism, which flourished in *The World of Art*, a periodical founded by the critic and impresario Sergei Diaghilev in 1898, to which the painter, theatrical designer and art historian Aleksandr Benois was a leading contributor. Art historians and painters, who cultivated links with writers of the new wave, discovered movements in foreign art and rediscovered old Russian traditions of painting and architecture. Numerous exhibitions of Russian painting were organized, both in Russia and abroad. Avant-garde movements in painting – Primitivism, Rayonism, Suprematism, Constructivism, Cubism, Futurism – flourished in the years leading up to and beyond the revolutions of 1917. A generation of Russian and Ukrainian painters, including Natal'ia Goncharova, Mikhail Larionov, Kasimir Malevich and Vasilii Kandinsky, established international reputations.[22] The Russian artistic renaissance found expression in music too, first with the late operas of Nikolai Rimsky-Korsakov and the compositions and recitals of Sergei Rachmaninov and Aleksandr Scriabin and then with the emergence of Igor' Stravinsky, who wrote scores for ballets produced by Diaghilev in Paris from 1909 up until the outbreak of the First World War.

Equally important, and interlinked with some of these artistic developments, was a new direction in Russian thought. By the late nineteenth century, the Orthodox Church had become discredited by its association with the autocratic regime, but in the Silver Age interest in Christianity revived in the intelligentsia. The religious renaissance found expression both among philosophers who at one time or another held academic positions, such as Nikolai Berdiaev and Sergei Bulgakov, and among creative artists, some of them associated with Symbolist circles, especially Dmitrii Merezhkovsky and his wife, the poetess Zinaida Gippius, who aimed to bring members of the intelligentsia together with representatives of the Orthodox clergy. Both wings of this movement produced influential publications. From the more academic wing came notable collections of essays, especially the famous volume entitled *Landmarks* (1909). The more artistic wing used a monthly review, *The New Way*, as a vehicle for the publication of proceedings of Religious-Philosophical Meetings which Merezhkovsky, Gippius and their friend Dmitrii Filosofov had organized in the years 1901–3. While members of the former group tried to restore traditional Christian values, to which some of them came after a youthful attachment to Marxism, members of the latter group sought new forms of spirituality. A void was also filled, in this new age of moral uncertainty, by unorthodox forms of belief, spiritualism and interest in the occult. As for the enduring influence of the great classical authors, none engaged the attention of writers and thinkers of the Silver Age more than Dostoevsky: Berdiaev, Merezhkovsky, the literary critic Vasilii Rozanov and the philosopher Lev Shestov all wrote about him at length.[23]

The literature and thought of the Russian Silver Age were deeply tinged with expectation of some final struggle – moral and religious, as well as political – between opposing forces and with a presentiment of apocalypse. Even a perusal of the titles of works by writers of this age confirms their fears about the end of an old civilization and their hopes of a new beginning.[24] This millenarian mood, which was felt by many Symbolists and religious philosophers, owed much to the Dostoevskian novel, especially *The Idiot* (1868) and *The Devils* (1871–2).[25] The spirit of the age is captured in Blok's enigmatic narrative poem 'The Twelve' (1918), at the end of which Jesus appears at the head of a platoon of Red Guards, who represent the working people, marching through St Petersburg in a snowstorm, ensuring that the 'old world' of the bourgeoisie will die.

Some fifty years after the October Revolution, Rand recalled that as a child she had caught 'a glimpse of the pre-World War I world, the last afterglow of the most radiant *cultural* atmosphere in human history', although she peevishly denied that Russia had had any part in this achievement of 'Western culture'.[26] Not that all, or even much, of the great cultural and intellectual experimentation of fin-de-siècle Europe and late imperial Russia could have appealed to Rand. In what purported to be a serious essay on aesthetics, written in 1971, she spoke of 'the silliness of the dots-and-dashes Impressionists' and derided abstract art as indicative of the 'disintegration of man's conceptual faculty'. She was similarly dismissive of 'so-called modern music', which she thought was '*not* music' at all.[27] In fact, she does not seem to have shown much open-minded appreciation of either the visual arts or music in general. Her comments on her husband's modest efforts at the easel suggest fixed and trite ideas about drawing and painting. Of the classical composers, she had a love of Rachmaninov, who was popular in Russia when she was growing up, but Beethoven she considered malevolent and Brahms worthless.

Her youthful preferences seem to have been light Italian opera and military marches.[28]

As for poetry, Rand's alter ego in *We the Living*, Kira Argounova (whose musical preference, incidentally, is for foxtrots) never reads it (*WL*: 249).[29] Rand herself cannot have shared the Symbolists' aestheticism, let alone their mystical assumptions about correspondences between the visible and invisible worlds. All the same, she seems indebted to them for their emancipation of the individual from social obligations and their rediscovery of Dostoevsky. Perhaps she had something in common with the Futurist Mayakovsky too, despite his communist sympathies. Certainly, it is achievements of the industrial age of the sort that Mayakovsky celebrated – in Rand's case, skyscrapers, steel-mills, oil-wells, railways, bridges and the motor car – that most readily aroused her to something approaching lyricism in her own writings. As regards the religious philosophy of the Silver Age, Rand's atheism would seem to preclude respect for it, although she may have been taught and influenced by a prominent representative of it, the neo-idealist Nikolai Lossky, while she was a student at Petrograd University.[30] Nonetheless, at some level she did share the expectation or hope of religious philosophers that a great transformation of human consciousness was imminent.

Intellectual and literary influences

No reader of Barbara Branden's biography of Rand would conclude that Rand's ideas and way of thinking were much affected by intellectual predecessors, bar a very small number who influenced her in some way and to some degree. On the contrary, Rand's thought and method of presenting it, if we are to believe Branden, would seem to have been worked out almost entirely in Rand's own precocious mind and fertile imagination during her childhood, adolescence and early womanhood. Certainly, readers will find no evidence in Branden's book that Rand was indebted to Russian writers or thinkers. She was dismissive, according to Branden, of the great classical authors who were studied at her secondary school. Alexander Pushkin, Turgenev,

Tolstoy, Chekhov – none answered to her particular taste. In later years, she detested Aleksandr Solzhenitsyn, who came to prominence in world literature in the 1960s, on account of his apparent yearning for theocratic government.[31]

Indeed, Rand viewed herself as an almost uniquely original and penetrating thinker. She was notoriously unwilling to admit to any intellectual debts, although she did acknowledge a small number, albeit in a highly qualified and more or less grudging way. 'The only philosophical debt I can acknowledge', she wrote in 1957 in her afterword to the first edition of *Atlas Shrugged*, 'is to Aristotle. I most emphatically disagree with a great many parts of his philosophy – but his definition of the laws of logic and of the means of human knowledge is so great an achievement that his errors are irrelevant by comparison' (*AS*: [1171]).

A decade later, in the introduction to an edition of *The Fountainhead* that marked the twenty-fifth anniversary of the first publication of that novel, she also paid a more equivocal compliment to Friedrich Nietzsche, with whose work *Thus Spoke Zarathustra* (1883–92) she first became acquainted through a cousin when she was a seventeen-year-old university student.[32] Despite Nietzsche's mysticism, irrationalism and flawed metaphysics and epistemology, Rand confessed that she did admire him as a 'poet' who at times managed to project 'a magnificent feeling for man's greatness, expressed in emotional, *not* intellectual, terms' (*F*: xii; Rand's italics). Like many Russian readers and writers of the Silver Age, Rand was undoubtedly affected by Nietzsche, especially by his conception of the Superman (*Übermensch*) unrestrained by conventional moral prohibitions. Nietzsche is quoted admiringly by her cynical egoist, the former aristocrat Leo Kovalensky, of whom she approves, in *We the Living* (*WL*: 122).[33]

Some of Nietzsche's ideas, including his anticipation of the human condition in a world without God or Christian morality, are prefigured in the writings of Dostoevsky, of which Nietzsche himself was aware and with which Rand also became acquainted during her university years. Rand acknowledged Dostoevsky's achievement in integrating 'an important theme with a complex plot structure', so that the events in his novels 'proceed from, express, illustrate and dramatize their themes'. She praised the depth of his study of motivation, which was illustrated by his ability in *Crime and Punishment* to reveal 'the soul of a criminal all the way down to his philosophical premises', and 'his merciless dissection of the psychology of evil'.[34] She valued his concern – which Dostoevsky shared with other writers Rand considered 'Romantic' – with moral values and their power to shape human character.[35] What she was most reluctant to acknowledge, we may suspect from such references to Dostoevsky as we find in her published and unpublished writings, was that this prophet of 'the Russian idea',[36] or indeed any Russian writer, had any influence upon her in the realm of *ideas*, as opposed to literary technique.[37] She was entitled to state, it is true, that Dostoevsky's philosophy and sense of life were 'almost diametrically opposed' to her own,[38] but she did appropriate from him and use for her own purposes ideas which Dostoevsky believed would have catastrophic consequences. She also emulated him in her habit of exploring ideas to their limits and of turning the ideas of others inside out and using them against their original exponents, and in attempting to write what can be called an apocalyptic novel.[39]

Intellectual and literary influence may of course be difficult to prove, owing not just to a writer's reluctance to acknowledge it but also to the need to differentiate between borrowing and adaptation and to consider whether use of the ideas and techniques of other writers is even conscious. When we come to explore the extent of Rand's indebtedness to Russian thinkers and writers we encounter a further difficulty. Most of the people who have had access to Rand's personal papers are not dispassionate scholars but keepers of her flame, such as her legal and intellectual heir, Leonard Peikoff. Her notebooks, published in a volume of over 700 pages in 1997 under the title *Journals of Ayn Rand*, copyright of which belongs to the Estate of Ayn Rand, are a particularly unreliable source of information. They have been edited in such a way that they amount to a cosmetic rewriting of Ayn Rand, rather than Rand's own writing.[40] Politically inconvenient or incorrect remarks about such matters as democracy, racial determinism and women have been excised from them.[41] The first part of the claim made by their editor, David Harriman, that 'the purpose of fiction writing', for Rand, was 'not to denounce that which one despises, but to exalt that which one admires', does not withstand the slightest scrutiny.[42] We may safely assume that such champions as Peikoff and Harriman are naturally disinclined to reveal intellectual debts, such as dependency on or conscious or unconscious borrowing from Russian sources that Rand herself did not want to acknowledge. For one thing, such debts might detract from the reputation for exceptional originality that Rand wished to cultivate. For another, they would make it possible to associate her with the intellectual and literary traditions of a nation abhorred by Rand herself and widely perceived by Americans as a major adversary of the United States. We therefore cannot expect to find in publications overseen by Rand's disciples such revealing information about the writer's reading habits and the ways in which they informed her literary creation as we would normally gather from reading the notebooks or personal correspondence of a writer. The dearth of reference to Russian writers in the published version of Rand's notebooks does not reliably tell us that Rand did not engage with them.

Given these difficulties in gathering explicit evidence about Rand's intellectual and literary debts, it is important to produce textual evidence of them from her writings. There are indeed many places in Rand's fiction where readers familiar with Russian literature and thought hear a more or less unmistakable echo of a passage, allusion, turn of phrase or concept from a pre-revolutionary Russian source. Echoes of the writings of Dostoevsky, which Rand, by her own admission, had read voraciously, have special value in an account of her association with the Russian intellectual and literary tradition. However, the utterances of Dostoevsky and his characters were not monological. They were responses to the ideas of other writers and thinkers in the polyphonic debate in which the Russian literary community and intelligentsia were engaged. For this reason, it is useful also to allude to ideas put forward by contemporaries of Dostoevsky which informed the impassioned debates that give meaning to the existence of his characters and life to his novels and which found their way, after further reworking, into Rand's novels.

Foremost among the thinkers against whom Dostoevsky pitted himself during the period following his return to St Petersburg in 1859, after almost ten years of imprisonment and Central Asian exile to which he had been sentenced for his youthful participation in circles that studied the writings of French utopian socialists, was the utilitarian, atheist and materialist Nikolai Chernyshevsky. One of the earliest Russian socialists, Chernyshevsky was the author of a novel, *What Is to Be Done?* (1863), which, although poorly written, enjoyed lasting popularity in Russian radical circles from the 1860s.[43] Another thinker with whose ideas Dostoevsky engaged was Dmitrii Pisarev, a prototypical 'nihilist', or 'realist' as Pisarev preferred to call fictional characters he admired, such as Evgenii Bazarov, the central character of Turgenev's novel *Fathers and Children* (1862). Pisarev echoed many of Chernyshevsky's ideas but gave them a more elitist turn and yet more destructive force. Like Dostoevsky's religious thought, the ideas of these radical thinkers remained highly topical in the early twentieth century, while Rand was still in Russia. After all, Chernyshevsky, Pisarev and many other radical thinkers who followed their examples in the 1860s and 1870s are commonly seen as intellectual forerunners of the revolutionaries who seized power in October 1917. We should add to the list of adversaries with whom Rand engages in her writings Karl Marx and Friedrich Engels, whose ideas, of course, provided the theoretical foundation for Bolshevik ideology. Although no explicit mention of Dostoevsky, Chernyshevsky, Pisarev or Marx's Russian disciple Lenin is to be found in *The Fountainhead* or *Atlas Shrugged*, the spirit of all of them lives on in those novels.

Identification of the Russian origin of many an idea advanced, attitude adopted or technique used by a writer who occupies such an important place in the American right-wing pantheon may prove disconcerting to admirers of Rand who consider her writings expressions of the essence of American identity. Certainly, knowledge of Rand's deployment of ideas formulated in another historical and political context by Russian thinkers of various political complexions should make us question whether the full import of her outlook has really been understood by her disciples. Rand's uncompromising atheism and hostility to Christianity and all its 'criminal, ludicrous, tragic nonsense'[44]; her reverence for self-designated elites; her rejection of the compromises on which democracy is necessarily built; her scant respect for laws or regulations that hinder her heroes' activity; her indifference to the family as the basic social unit; her permissive sexual mores – all these positions seem wholly at variance with some of the values and traditions that conservative American patriots tend, on the face of it, to uphold. The Russian radical intelligentsia, on the other hand, would have been entirely comfortable with them.

CHAPTER 2

RAND AND THE RUSSIAN INTELLECTUAL TRADITION

The Russian intelligentsia and its outlook

Throughout the nineteenth century, Russia was governed by an oppressive autocratic regime which exercised censorship of publications through multiple agencies and under which political questions could not often be discussed freely. Periods in which reforms were promised or attempted, such as the early years of the reigns of both Alexander I (1801–25) and Alexander II (1855–81), alternated with periods characterized by repression or reactionary policies, such as the 'seven dismal years' with which the reign of Nicholas I (1825–55) ended, following the revolutionary disturbances in Europe in 1848–9, and the reign of Alexander III, after the assassination of Alexander II. And yet, despite this stifling political atmosphere, late imperial Russia saw its national culture and intellectual life come into full bloom.

From around the 1840s, this flowering was stimulated by the growth of a Russian diaspora. Dissident émigrés could freely express their views in uncensored publications, such as Alexander Herzen's *Bell*, which was produced on his Free Russian Press in London over the years 1857–65 and then in Geneva for two more years. Most importantly, Russia found its voice and identity through the magnificent development of a national literature which gave hope to humane, educated men and women as a 'ray of light in the kingdom of darkness'.[1] Whereas in the 1820s and 1830s Pushkin, whose many-sided œuvre is of seminal importance in Russian literature, had presided over a golden age of poetry, in the 1840s a golden age of prose began. In the space of some forty years, Nikolai Gogol', Ivan Goncharov, Turgenev, Dostoevsky and Tolstoy produced all (or, in Tolstoy's case, most) of their major works. These and many other writers of prose fiction developed the Russian novel as a medium for the exploration of timeless emotional, psychological and moral matters of universal significance, but they also turned it into a vehicle in which debate about the nation's contemporary social and political life, lacking other fora, could be conducted and in which writers could speculate on Russia's grand historical destiny.

Classical Russian prose fiction developed together with a corpus of thought on aesthetic, moral, theological, psychological, social and political questions. Examples of such writing appeared alongside serialized works of fiction in dedicated sections of the so-called 'thick journals', such as *The Contemporary* and *Notes of the Fatherland*, which played a crucial part in Russian literary and intellectual life from the mid-nineteenth century.[2] This corpus of non-fictional prose printed in periodical publications in late imperial Russia is classified as *publitsistika*, defined in Russian lexicography as 'literature on the socio-political questions of the present day'.[3] The term is often rendered in English as 'publicism', but in truth this word is not widely used in English to denote topical journalism.

From around the 1860s, the group that created the tradition of socio-political debate in the periodical press, together with their readers and members of certain emergent professions (especially teachers, medical workers and employees of the local councils that were set up after the reform of local government in the mid-1860s), came to be known as the intelligentsia.[4] This distinctive element of Russia's embryonic civil society offered a framework for new kinds of contacts across boundaries of ethnicity and religion.[5] Its members also came from different social strata. If in the early stages of the development of the intelligentsia nobles played a prominent part, by the age of Alexander II men of non-noble origin, so-called *raznochintsy*, came to the fore, especially members of a sub-group known jocularly as *popovichi* (sons of priests), whose number included Chernyshevsky. What distinguished the intelligentsia, though, was not social origin but shared belief in the importance of a vigorous intellectual and cultural life for the nation, commitment to socio-political ideas, a social conscience and concern for the public interest. By the early twentieth century, this social group – which would be replicated in other modernizing countries, in Europe and beyond – had become such a distinctive and influential feature of the nation's life that the Russian term itself (*intelligentsiia*) began to enter other lexicons, including the English.[6]

Although the Russian intelligentsia cannot be altogether equated with the nation's literary community, in many cases the same individual (Herzen, Dostoevsky and Tolstoy are examples) was both a creative writer and a polemical journalist, commentator on current affairs, or pamphleteer. Creative writers in late imperial Russia generally shared the sense of civic duty and high moral purpose of members of the intelligentsia. Again, both tended, by virtue of their intellectual independence, to find themselves at a distance from power in a polity that was intolerant of pluralism. At the same time, both acquired power of another sort – the cultural and moral authority of a group that aspired, like Tolstoy, to express the conscience of the nation and whose members were liable to suffer persecution as the price of integrity. Irrespective of where we draw the dividing line between artists and intelligentsia, representatives of a broad range of political opinion were to be found among both types of writer, from conservative nationalist to liberal and revolutionary socialist.

From these many political vantage points, Russian thinkers and writers addressed an array of 'accursed questions' (*prokliatye voprosy*) that could not be productively discussed in the political bodies of the Russian Empire, at least until short-lived parliamentary institutions, or *dumy*, were set up in the wake of the revolution of 1905. Some of these questions were essentially aesthetic. What purposes is art supposed to serve, and what sort of literature and literary forms meet the needs of a society in a state of flux? Some fell within ethics, the branch of philosophy concerned with human character and conduct. Into what categories might human individuals be divided, and should they prioritize their own interests or subordinate or sacrifice their personal self for others? Many related to economic organization or social justice and thus fell within the broad domain of political philosophy. Who should own natural resources, such as land and minerals, and the facilities, such as farms and mines, that are required to exploit them? Should the products of human labour, mental and physical, be distributed to each according to her or his needs? Many Russian thinkers were also intensely interested in the philosophy of history and questions which had geopolitical significance. Did nations and societies develop in a random way or according to some teleological purpose or in conformity with iron laws? The answers to such questions informed debate about what sort of political activity, if any, was needed. Would a new order come into being through governmental agency or through some moral transformation which led a sufficient number of individuals to conduct their relations with fellow-humans in a new way?

Dwelling on such questions and reflecting on their interconnection, many Russian thinkers attempted to construct a grand intellectual system. At the highest level, such a system would accommodate compatible positions in different branches of philosophy, especially aesthetics, ethics and politics but not excluding metaphysics. The Russian term for the kind of system that the intelligentsia aspired to construct, *mirovozzrenie* (a world-outlook), points to the scope and ambition of the project and even to the affinity of the concept with the products of the German intellectual world (the term is a loan-translation of the German *Weltanschauung*). A 'world-outlook' was a systematic philosophy of life containing both a supposedly infallible description of the first principles of nature, thought and knowledge and speculation on what ought to be. It promised a certainty, consistency and intelligibility that could be satisfying, indeed reassuring to an unsettled spirit.

Unfamiliar as the concept might be to readers brought up in an anglophone intellectual tradition and jarring as the German and Russian terms and the English translation of them might seem to English-speakers, a world-outlook was precisely what Rand wished to construct as her tool for engaging with the 'accursed questions' that animated her. She seeks to present readers with a theory of everything, a comprehensive and coherent set of beliefs about human needs and wants, behaviour, ambitions, economic activity and political life, a 'philosophy' which her prose fiction is designed to expound.[7] Eventually, she came to call this doctrine 'Objectivism', the main principles of which, according to the ARI website, are 'reason, rational self-interest and laissez-faire capitalism'. Evidently, it was above all this ability of Rand's to present, as Barbara Branden put it, 'a total world view and a systematic philosophical system of awesome logical consistency'[8] that made her writing so appealing to her acolytes and that seemed so original to people who were unaware of the Russian provenance of her way of thinking.

There are two other respects in which Rand had an affinity with the Russian intelligentsia, especially the radical wing of it which laid theoretical foundations for the development of the Russian revolutionary movement and thus played a major part in undermining the old autocratic regime.

First, although she liked to associate herself with the Romantic literary tradition, Rand had a positivistic mindset. The leading members of the radical intelligentsia, by and large, claimed to recognize only that which could be verified or shown to be true by means of logic, mathematics or scientific method. They set great store by the natural sciences, such as physics, chemistry, zoology, geology and medicine, and by the empirical methods that enabled scientists to establish facts and formulate laws of nature, demolishing unproven assumptions or cherished prejudices in the process. They also embraced the social sciences (sociology, criminology, psychology, anthropology and so forth) that were coming into being in late-nineteenth-century Europe and in which the rigorous method of the natural sciences was expected to be extended to the study of human society and behaviour. Rand, for her part, enjoyed and excelled at school in mathematics and the natural sciences.[9] Her novels bristle with reference to and admiration of scientific and technological discovery and achievement. Her first heroine, Kira Argounova, hopes to become an engineer. Dagny Taggart, her heroine in *Atlas Shrugged*, would also seem to be representing her creator when Rand, describing Dagny's childhood, explains that she loved the sciences, especially mathematics, because they are 'so clean, so strict, so luminously rational' (*AS*: 51). The curriculum of the innovative university course that the world-changing heroes of *Atlas Shrugged* have undergone under the guidance of two outstanding teachers (Robert Stadler and Hugh Akston) in a once-prestigious American university included natural science as well as philosophy.

Second, Rand emitted the behavioural signals associated with the 'nihilist' (*nigilist*, or feminine *nigilistka*) who dramatically appeared in the Russian intelligentsia in the 1860s. An intellectual iconoclast, she was willing to offend religious sensibilities. Like nihilists again (but quite unlike most American readers of the 1930s and 1940s[10]), she vociferously insisted on sexual freedom irrespective of marital status. She thought of her prolonged affair with Nathaniel Branden as a perfectly rational arrangement which needed to be discussed with her husband and Nathaniel's wife and to which only irrational and morally deficient partners would object.[11] Her provocative outspokenness, her delight in shocking listeners or readers, her heavy smoking (which also served in her new habitat as an indicator of American identity) – all these signals would have been recognizable to the young men and women of late imperial Russia who displayed their rejection of conventional norms through their conduct and dress as well as through acceptance of new ideas that scandalized conventional society.

The intelligentsia's way of thinking and writing

Besides considering a wide range of 'accursed questions' and trying to address them within a comprehensive intellectual system, the Russian intelligentsia also conducted its debates in a manner, style and tone which students of late imperial Russian fiction and socio-political journalism will recognize in Rand's fiction.

For one thing, contemporary social, political and economic issues were usually discussed in a partisan, vituperative way. Participants in journalistic debate wrote in a self-righteous, 'accusatory' tone, as if only members of one school of thought could be expressing views that were correct, morally acceptable and sincerely held. Their posture brooked no compromise, and they showed no inclination to search for middle ground. Echoes of this censorious tone can be heard everywhere in the utterances of Rand's heroes. As John Galt, her incarnation of the perfect human being, tells the American nation: 'There are two sides to every issue: one side is right and the other is wrong, but the middle is always evil' (*AŚ*: 1054). As for fictional characters who think differently from Rand's mouthpieces, their utterances are introduced with contempt: they gibber, grunt, snarl, snivel, whine or yell. Writers with whom Rand disagreed, or their works, are described in her notebooks as 'dishonest, disgraceful, stinking', 'idiotic' or 'disgusting'. No neutrality, in short, is acceptable in Rand's world, and she was unapologetic about what she admitted was her 'unforgiving tone of moral indignation'.[12]

The ideological outlook of members of the radical intelligentsia in late imperial Russia was typically built (as, perhaps, ideological systems generally are) with the help of simplistic binary philosophical and rhetorical oppositions. At least five oppositions strike a chord for students of the Russian intelligentsia who come across Rand's writings: a moral opposition between altruism and egoism (though Rand reverses the normal association of these polarities with good and evil respectively); the contrast between extraordinary men and women, the elite, on the one hand, and ordinary humans, the common herd or mob, on the other; the contrast between the belief that humans have free will and determinism, that is to say the belief that human actions are caused by factors over which individual men and women have no control; the opposition between the individual and the collective, a political issue which Rand considered 'the greatest, most urgent conflict' of her time[13]; and an opposition of a geopolitical nature between a homeland (for Rand, America became this) and everywhere else.

More generally, Rand sustains a straightforward binary opposition throughout *The Fountainhead* and *Atlas Shrugged* between 'them', the innumerable ideological foes about whom her heroes speak contemptuously, and 'us', her heroes themselves. In the first of these novels, the principal opposition is between Peter Keating and Ellsworth Toohey (insincere humans who lead inauthentic lives), on the one hand, and Howard Roark (Rand's example, in this novel, of a human who lives life as it should be lived, she supposes), on the other. In *Atlas Shrugged*, 'they' are represented by James Taggart (the nominal head of the failing railway company, Taggart Transcontinental, whose fortunes are central to the novel's plot), Robert Stadler (a scientist of genius who has placed his gift at the service of the now corrupted American state) and a host of secondary characters whose main function is to trivialize or otherwise discredit ideas Rand deplores. 'We', Rand's elite, are led by her nonpareil, John Galt, and his ideologically pure associates Francisco d'Anconia (the heir to the fortune of a family of South American copper magnates) and Ragnar Danneskjöld (the descendant of a Norwegian noble family). In due course, Galt, Francisco and Ragnar also win over the self-driven industrialist Hank Rearden (the inventor of a remarkable new alloy), James Taggart's equally highly motivated sister Dagny (the *de facto* leader of Taggart Transcontinental) and less conscious but instinctive loyalists such as Dagny's assistant Eddie Willers.

There is also plentiful evidence in Rand's writing of the messianism that had coloured Russian thought and literature in the Silver Age. The world presented in *Atlas Shrugged*, Francisco points out, has reached a great and final moral crisis which is 'the climax of centuries of evil', and it falls to 'men of the mind' like Galt, Ragnar and himself to 'put an end to it, once and for all, or perish' (*AS*: 619). If they succeed in their mission, then Rand's heroes will bring about a 'Second Renaissance' (*AS*: 637), albeit a Renaissance 'not of oil paintings and cathedrals – but of oil derricks, power plants, and motors made of Rearden Metal' (*AS*: 249).

Rand addresses questions, then, that were extensively debated by Russian thinkers and writers, adopts a similarly confrontational stance, makes use of authorial techniques they had habitually employed and strikes a millenarian tone that is often heard in their writing. At the same time, she radically re-evaluates certain qualities that many of those thinkers and writers prized. Prominent among the qualities by which Russian intellectuals set great store, but which Rand tries to undermine, is selflessness. Self-sacrifice was highly esteemed both by the atheistic Russian radical intelligentsia and by Orthodox Christians such as Dostoevsky. As a rule, valorization of selflessness and self-sacrifice was bound up with a powerful sense of duty to serve some ideal higher than the individual ego. Among the revolutionary Populists in the latter part of the nineteenth century, this sense found expression in the feeling best articulated by Petr Lavrov in his celebrated *Historical Letters* (1869) that the 'critically thinking minority' had a moral debt (*dolg*; the word also means 'duty') to discharge to the common people, at whose expense members of the minority had had the opportunity to develop themselves intellectually and culturally.[14] To Rand's heroes, on the other hand, the concept of duty was incomprehensible[15] and the notion of moral obligation to others intolerable. 'The word that has destroyed you', Galt tells the nation, is '*sacrifice*' (*AS*: 1027–8; Rand's italics).

Another particularly striking example of Rand's reversal of the ethos traditionally valued by Russian thinkers and writers concerns attitudes towards money. Members of the intelligentsia strove as a matter of honour to present themselves as unmercenary. Thinkers at different points on the political spectrum, from socialists such as Herzen, the literary critic Vissarion Belinsky and Chernyshevsky on the left to conservatives such as Dostoevsky on the right, condemned cupidity and deplored what they saw as the bourgeois ethic of thrift and assiduity.[16] Rand's 'men of superlative ability' like Hank Rearden, who have made their fortunes 'by personal effort', on the other hand, resentfully demand their financial deserts, which they believe are limitless, and refuse to apologize for their success or their fortunes (*AS*: 480). Ragnar, aided by a mole in a Washington tax office, is compiling a record of all the money extorted from such men 'in hidden taxes, in regulations, in wasted time, in lost effort, in energy spent to overcome artificial obstacles', so that it can be returned to its rightful owners when the revolution that Rand's heroes are plotting has taken place (*AS*: 578–80).

Most memorably, the making of money is glorified and identified as Americans' finest contribution to human civilization. Francisco uses a speech at a wedding reception (!) to try to convince the assembled guests that money is the 'barometer of society's virtue', 'the base of a moral existence', a guarantee of objective standards. He can pay no more reverential tribute to the United States than to say that it is '*a country of money*' and consequently 'a country of reason, justice, freedom, production, achievement'. It is 'the proudest distinction of Americans', he believes (mistakenly), 'that they were the people who created the phrase "to *make* money"', an expression which for Rand captures 'the essence of human morality'.[17] Far from being the root of all evil, as another character has averred shortly before Francisco begins to speak, money is 'the root of all good' (*AS*: 410–15). Thus Rand, far from agreeing with the numerous Russian writers who considered it ignoble to be actuated by hope of mercenary reward, believes that Americans should 'choose to wear the sign of the dollar on [their] foreheads, proudly, as [their] badge of nobility' (*AS*: 684). It is apt that the dollar sign should be used as the logo of a luxury brand of cigarettes (a vital commodity for Americans in Rand's novels) produced for the elite in the utopian community founded by her heroes in *Atlas Shrugged*. She herself would proudly wear a brooch in the form of a dollar sign.

The novel as a vehicle for philosophical polemic

The ways of thinking and writing that were ingrained in the polemics of the Russian intelligentsia by the time Rand became engrossed in philosophical, political and social questions offered, in sum, a framework that suited her very well for the expression of her intransigent mind and personality. Moral issues were central in the Russian intellectual model, as they would be in Rand's own writings. Choices tended to be conceived as having a bearing on the outcome of an epic struggle between good and evil. The answer to any question might be found within an integrated intellectual system in which all elements were interdependent and mutually consistent. The answers the system supplied had the status of truths which could be embraced with a certainty that was reassuring in a fast-changing world where values were in flux. Those who were abreast of the latest intellectual fashion were entitled to preach the new truths and values uncompromisingly and to despise anyone who disputed them.

However, Rand owed a debt to the Russian intelligentsia and literary community for even more than their identification of certain key questions, their preoccupation with the construction of intellectual systems, and their method and style of argumentation. She was also indebted to them for nurturing a tradition of prose fiction in which the ideas animating the intelligentsia were embodied in literary characters and dramatized as ways of living. In short, Russian forerunners had led the way in novelizing thought and in creating the foundations for a sub-genre of the novel, namely the novel of ideas. There were canonical Russian contributions to this sub-genre which Rand undoubtedly knew, such as Turgenev's *Fathers and Children*, Chernyshevsky's *What Is to Be Done?*, Dostoevsky's *Crime and Punishment* (1866), *The Devils* and *The Brothers Karamazov* (1879–80) and Tolstoy's *Resurrection* (1899).

Fiction, Barbara Branden observed correctly, but without reference to Rand's familiarity with Russian culture, 'made possible the integration of wide abstract principles and their direct expression in and application to man's life'. Rand 'wanted to define a moral ideal, to present her kind of man – and to project, through fiction, the living reality of that ideal'.[18] By the time she was eighteen, writing stories was firmly linked in her mind with presenting philosophical ideas. In maturity she saw herself as a novelist-philosopher and refused to accept that either of her roles had primacy.[19] However, she did not arrive at this conception of the novel as a vehicle for illustrating what it means in practice to hold certain ideas merely by exercising unique powers of reasoning and imagination. On the contrary, her prose fiction and her remarks about it constantly bear witness to engagement with the Russian tradition of reflection on aesthetic matters of which no intelligent person educated in early twentieth-century St Petersburg and Petrograd could have been unaware. What was 'The Aesthetic Relationship of Art to Reality', as Chernyshevsky had asked in a master's dissertation published in 1855? What is art (in a broad sense of the word that includes literature), as Tolstoy famously enquired in 1897 in a tract with that title? Was art a means to an end or an end in itself?

In fact, it was in the domain of aesthetics that some of the earliest skirmishes between factions in the intelligentsia took place in mid-nineteenth-century Russia. The intellectual rebellion led by

Chernyshevsky began with his rejection, in his dissertation, of the view then prevailing in Russia that the artist's mission was to provide access to a transcendent realm of beauty – a view derived from Plato's notion that beyond the imperfect visible world there lies a world of perfect forms which is inaccessible to most mortals at most times. Rather, the artist's purpose, as Chernyshevsky defined it, was to reproduce the mundane world of everyday human experience.[20] Writers guided by Chernyshevsky would therefore turn their attention to current social problems and counter the pessimistic view that humans – like many a character in Turgenev's fiction, for example – should accept contemporary reality and a tragic personal fate with resignation. And yet, although Chernyshevsky encouraged a view of art as mere reproduction of reality, he himself also used the novel as a tool with which to spur readers into refashioning reality. The 'new people' he created in *What Is to Be Done?* look ahead to the sort of society in which they would willingly live and prepare to make a future of their own choice.

Chernyshevsky also stimulated a utilitarian brand of literary criticism. The most distinguished representatives of such criticism were Nikolai Dobroliubov, a close colleague of Chernyshevsky's at *The Contemporary*, and Pisarev, whose writings, including an article on 'The Destruction of Aesthetics' (1865), attacked the doctrine of 'art for art's sake', according to which the creator of 'true' art sets out with no social or political intention.[21] To critics belonging to the utilitarian school, a work of fiction was to be valued primarily on account of its content, not its artistry or stylistic elegance. Russian radical criticism thus helped to prepare the ground for acceptance of the use of art as a tool of propaganda, for which purpose the new Soviet state began to exploit it in the early 1920s, around the time when Rand was studying at the University of Petrograd.[22]

Insofar as novelists hold views that they wish to promote in their fiction, they may need to create exemplary characters who can articulate their ideas and show readers what will happen, they hope, when those ideas are put into practice – hence the emergence in Russian literature, in the age of Alexander II, of the 'positive hero', a decisive man of action who is usually of lower social origin than nobles and who has set himself a clear goal and is capable of fighting for a cause.[23] From the pen of a great literary talent, characters in the novel of ideas, such as Turgenev's Bazarov, Dostoevsky's Rodion Raskol'nikov in *Crime and Punishment* and Ivan Karamazov in *The Brothers Karamazov*, all of whom embody ideas on which their sense of their life's meaning depends, emerge as vivid, multi-dimensional and often tragic literary creations. However, these characters are in some way flawed and, as a result, plausibly human. Once it becomes an author's purpose to present a flawless 'positive' hero, then literary veracity may be jeopardized, as is the case with Turgenev's Bulgarian patriot Insarov in *On the Eve* (1860). The clearest instantiations of positive heroes as wooden, implausible mouthpieces for the views of Russian authors, especially authors of lesser literary talent, are the proto-revolutionary Rakhmetov and his accomplices, Lopukhov and Kirsanov, who attempt to put Chernyshevsky's ethical doctrine of rational egoism into practice in *What Is to Be Done?*

That is not at all to say that the effectiveness of a literary character as a role model is necessarily diminished in the perception of readers seeking validation of their ideological position if that character is widely felt to be implausible. After all, readers apply differing aesthetic standards and read literary works in different ways. At any rate, bad writing (*plokhopis'* in Russian) does not seem inevitably to weaken the power of a work of fiction to influence readers in its own day or later times. Chernyshevsky's *What Is to Be Done?* has notorious literary weaknesses of the sort that numerous readers also find in Rand's novels (unbelievable characters and plot, stilted dialogue and tedious exposition of ideas), but it still moved many young Russian radicals to live in communes in the 1860s and 1870s. It also provided sustenance to Lenin, who read it repeatedly as a guide to life in the years after his elder brother, Aleksandr Ul'ianov, had been hanged, in May 1887, for plotting in that year to assassinate Alexander III. Lenin paid tribute to Chernyshevsky by reusing the title of his novel in one of his own key works, published in 1902. Bad writing, then, may prove very influential, as suggested by the title of Adam Weiner's book on the contribution of Rand's ideas to the adoption of policies that led to the international financial crisis of 2009.[24] Indeed, it may have particular appeal at times when a culture that prizes refinement and elegance in language, art and manners is being challenged, as was Russian noble culture in the period when Chernyshevsky wrote *What Is to Be Done?*, or when a political order is altogether breaking down, as was imperial Russia in the early twentieth century.

Questions of the sort that preoccupied Chernyshevsky, Dobroliubov, Pisarev and many Russian novelists about the writer's purpose, the relative importance of form and content, and characterization are always in Rand's mind. She roundly rejected Plato and the philosophical basis he provided for art for art's sake.[25] Her meticulous study of subjects such as architecture and railway construction attests to the care she took to root her novels in contemporary reality. She constantly engaged with ideas that seemed to shape the world around her. Her sense of her mission as an artist was optimistic, in that she saw the 'motive and purpose' of her writing as '*the projection of an ideal man*' (*F*: ix; Rand's italics). Her positive heroes provide readers with an example of how to live, which, if properly followed, might transform their environment to their advantage. Her authorial task was urgent, moreover, because at the time she was writing – the mid-twentieth century, when the American way of life was supposedly being undermined by communist infiltrators – humans had never so desperately 'needed a projection of things as they ought to be' (*F*: vii). She is quite prepared to prioritize ideological content over artistry – and rightly so, she might have felt, for artistry is unseemly in a prosaic age when the best men should be inspired by a futuristic vision of rapid industrialization, technological innovation and pitiless entrepreneurialism. Her novels may even strike readers as brazen examples of bad writing, produced for an age of iconoclasm in which *plokhopis'* is a virtue. Familiar with the early Russian examples of the novel of ideas and the aesthetic debates surrounding them, Rand went on to make contributions of her own to this sub-genre at the very time when other classic examples of it were coming out in the anglophone and francophone worlds.

CHAPTER 3
RAND AND RUSSIAN LITERARY MODELS

Rand as a dystopian novelist

The first two of Rand's works of prose fiction to be published belong to the sub-genre of the dystopian novel, which is a variety of the novel of ideas. Her first novel, *We the Living*, is the nearest thing she would produce, Rand said, to an autobiographical novel, in the sense that the ideas, convictions and values of her heroine, Kira Argounova, are Rand's own. At the same time, *We the Living* is an account of the worst sort of society Rand could imagine, a protest against the emerging communist autocracy from which she had fled and, more generally, against 'any dictatorship, anywhere, at any time'.[1] Under dictatorship, those rare beings who value their unique human self, like Kira and her two lovers, the rash egoist Leo Kovalensky and the staunch communist Andrei Taganov, can take one of three paths. They may try to protect their sense of life by escaping, like Kira, who dies in the attempt, or Rand herself, who succeeded (without official hindrance). They may engage in reckless resistance, in which case they will either be crushed or surrender their moral integrity, as does Leo. Or they may commit suicide, like Andrei, who thus demonstrates a certain heroism despite his cardinal ideological error, in Rand's eyes, of attachment to communist ideals.

Rand's second piece of prose fiction, the novelette *Anthem*, is even more overtly dystopian. Her hero in this short work, in which human individuals are treated as ciphers, is Equality 7-2521. He stands out as an intellectually gifted heretic who refuses to accept the view of the collectivist 'City' into which he has been born that all men and women (who refer to themselves as 'we') are one and indistinguishable from their fellows. Equality 7-2521 escapes to an 'Uncharted Forest' where, with a similarly heretical young woman, he will re-establish the free spirit of humans who lived in the distant 'Unmentionable Times' and revive the creative ego which the City has almost succeeded in stamping out. Rand herself attributed much importance to this work, once calling it her manifesto, her profession of faith and the essence of her entire philosophy.[2]

Like the novel of ideas in general, the dystopian novel began to flourish in the anglophone world from the second quarter of the twentieth century. Aldous Huxley's *Brave New World* (1932) and George Orwell's *Animal Farm* (1945) and *1984* (1949) are examples of it published in the period in which Rand was working on her own main works of prose fiction. However, this variety of the novel had Russian antecedents on which Rand evidently drew, or at least there were passages in Russian fiction which anticipated it. One such passage dealt with the collectivist community imagined by Shigalev in Dostoevsky's most overtly political novel, *The Devils*. Starting from a quest for 'unlimited freedom', Shigalev arrives at the perplexing conclusion that there must be 'unlimited despotism'.[3] Shigalev's finding is taken up in *The Fountainhead* by Rand's arch-villain Toohey, who masquerades as a liberal humanitarian with a social conscience but is in fact a power-hungry man who aspires to rule the world. 'Only by accepting total compulsion', Toohey says, 'can we achieve total freedom' (*F*: 579). Toohey predicted that 'freaks' such as Roark would still occasionally be born, but just as Shigalev foresaw the silencing of a Cicero, a Copernicus or a Shakespeare,[4] so Toohey would not expect such exceptional individuals to 'survive' beyond their twelfth year (presumably because they would be exterminated; *F*: 665–8). Another Dostoevskian model for Rand's dystopias is the community imagined by Ivan Karamazov in his 'poem', 'The Legend of the Grand Inquisitor', which Ivan relates to his brother Alesha in one of the early climaxes of *The Brothers Karamazov*. In this prophetic vision of totalitarianism, humans would gratefully trade their freedom for security and a reliable supply of bread.[5] Preaching the ideal of selflessness, which the masses will never be able to live up to, Rand's Toohey and a handful of other men of his ilk will also enjoy unlimited power, like the Grand Inquisitor.

Rand's most important Russian model for a dystopian state, though, was Evgenii Zamiatin's novel *We* (1924) in which subject D-503 rebels, unsuccessfully, against a dictatorial One State of the twenty-third century which immures itself within a protective Green Wall and obliterates individuality. It has to be said that Rand's *Anthem*, as others have pointed out, is 'extremely reminiscent' of Zamiatin's novel.[6] Although Zamiatin completed *We* in 1921, the full Russian text of the novel was not published until 1952 (and then in New York), because of its unpalatability in Soviet Russia. However, Rand may have been familiar with it much earlier, even before its first publication in English translation in 1924 and the appearance of extracts of the Russian text in Prague in 1927, for it was already circulating in Russian literary circles in the early 1920s. She would certainly have known it from one or more of these sources by the time she wrote *Anthem*.[7]

The Fountainhead and *Atlas Shrugged* have many more dimensions than *We the Living* or *Anthem*, but they too are at bottom dystopian novels. In the former, Roark fears that America may soon cease to exist in its previous, ideal state now that it has followed Europe in succumbing to a 'collectivism' that 'has brought men to a level of intellectual indecency never equaled on earth', a 'scale of horror without precedent' (*F*: 716–17). In *Atlas Shrugged*, America is ceasing to function effectively at the time when the novel opens (a time which Rand does not specify). Even in the shoppers' paradise of Fifth Avenue in New York, a quarter of the stores have gone out of business and their windows are 'dark and empty' (*AS*: 4–5). The city's Queensborough Bridge is closed for repairs and the Texas-Western Railroad has just gone bankrupt (*AS*: 12). Few people in the United States seem capable of doing their job adequately (*AS*: 329). The country's productivity is declining, and the spirit of its pioneering golden age has been lost.

As Herzen had famously asked in a novel of the 1840s in which he presented an unedifying account of the lethargic, amoral gentry leading futile lives in provincial Russia under Nicholas I, who is to blame for the dystopian state of affairs that the novelist observes?[8] Part of the blame for America's plight, Rand thinks, lies with all those responsible for what she perceives as the anti-individualistic turn in public opinion and government around the middle of the twentieth century. The intense anti-communism that derived from her family's experience in revolutionary Russia was bolstered by her conviction that communists had taken over the literary world of New York, where she had settled with her husband at the end of 1934. Totalitarianism, she wrote in a letter of 1940 or 1941 that she hoped would be distributed among 'all innocent fifth-columnists', had 'already won a complete victory in many American minds and conquered all of our intellectual life'.[9] Her political consciousness was sharpened by the activity she began to undertake as a propagandist for Republican causes. When the Democrat Roosevelt stood (successfully) for re-election for a third term of office in 1940, for instance, she campaigned energetically for his Republican opponent Wendell Willkie.[10]

Rand's fictional state in *Atlas Shrugged* may therefore be seen as the dystopian outcome of government by Democrats, who had extended the role of federal government and had all too willingly pursued policies of the sort, so it seemed to Rand, that had resulted in totalitarianism in her native country. Her fictional American state had set up innumerable bureaucratic institutions (the Bureau of Economic Planning and National Resources, the Unification Board, the Railroad Pool and so forth) to implement federal policy. It appeared also to be introducing a planned economy of the kind that had been imposed in the USSR, where five-year plans had been drawn up from 1928. 'Every expert', claims Dr Floyd Ferris, whose ideas and values readers of *Atlas Shrugged* realize they should distrust, 'has conceded long ago that a planned economy achieves the maximum of productive efficiency and that centralization leads to super-industrialization' (*AS*: 544). Following the example of the Communist Party of the Soviet Union, Rand's fictitious American government had taken to intervening in every area of economic life, dictating how industrial, commercial, manufacturing and business establishments should operate and what workers should produce and earn (*AS*: 538–9).

The dystopian turn towards socialism and communism is associated in Rand's mind with acceptance of the notion of the public or common good. In a 'Manifesto of Individualism' that she wrote in 1941, she bluntly stated that this notion was 'utterly evil',[11] and in *Atlas Shrugged* she discredits it by having characters and institutions she plainly abhors uphold it. James Taggart, for example, insists 'that the interests of society as a whole must always be placed first in any business undertaking' (*AS*: 22). Philanthropic organizations pester the wealthy for donations. Newspapers employ a 'humanitarian clique' of columnists to orchestrate criticism of wealth-creators who are driven by the profit motive (*AS*: 316, 476).

In short, Rand does not tolerate humanitarian concern or attempts to mitigate the harsh social effects of unregulated capitalism. She excludes 'questions of social welfare' from consideration of economic issues; the only factor that weighs with her super-entrepreneur Hank Rearden is the market for his metal (*AS*: 180). No public project funded by taxation produces results of which the heroes of her novels approve, whether it be the provision of affordable social housing, which enrages Roark in *The Fountainhead* (*F*: 605), or the outcomes of state-funded scientific research in *Atlas Shrugged*. Nor will she support any state intervention that might limit the freedom of action of capitalist industrialists and entrepreneurs by enabling 'the little fellow' to form 'leagues, cooperatives, associations' (*AS*: 349). She would have rejected out of hand the twenty-first-century view that corporations have a duty to ensure the health, safety and well-being of their employees or those who live in the vicinity of their plants, or to protect the natural environment. Least of all will she accept the right of the state to impose taxes on her hyperactive heroes. Rand finds dystopia, then, not only in places where a totalitarian regime enslaves a majority but also in places where concern for the general well-being limits the freedom of action of the small minority who care only for themselves. It follows that her utopia will be a far cry from classical Russian models, whether Christian or socialist, which preferred peaceful brotherly cooperation to aggressive competition between individual egos.

If the proximate causes of America's degeneration are the development of the notion of public interest among the nation's industrialists, bankers and politicians and the implementation of socialist or social-democratic policies by federal government at the behest of the scheming 'gangs' of the Washington elite (AS: 383), at a deeper level the blame for America's plight lies with 'intellectuals'. Rand does not use this word in quite the sense that it normally has in the anglophone world, where it tends to bring to mind people of high intelligence whose work or lives revolve around the study or application of complex ideas. What she has in mind is a broader group more akin to the socially and politically committed intelligentsia she knew from her Russian upbringing, a group she berated in terms of which populist conservatives engaged in today's culture wars surely approve. She had already taken aim at that intelligentsia in *We the Living*, in which a character whom she portrays with affection describes this socio-intellectual group as 'spineless, snivelling, impotent, blabbering, broad-minded, [and] drooling' (*WL*: 22).

Rand's 'intellectuals', reincarnated from the 1930s in an American setting, do include philosophers. Indeed, the worst culprits are evidently teachers of philosophy and social sciences at the tertiary level of the educational system. Hank Rearden, having witnessed the death of a young man killed by rioters at his metal mill and having himself been clubbed unconscious by a rioter, has no doubt about who, in the final analysis, is to blame. It is not so much the unknown thugs who committed these acts or the 'looting bureaucrats' who had hired them; it is 'the soft, safe assassins of college classrooms', 'the professors, the philosophers, the moralists' who had released the thugs upon the world (AS: 994, 997). The sound-minded union leader Fred Kinnan is of the same opinion. It is the 'intellectuals' (he uses the word repeatedly and sneeringly) who have delivered 'every country of Europe, one after another, to committees of goons'. Even the 'lousiest wharf rat in the longshoremen's union' is 'liable to remember suddenly that he is a man', but the intellectuals will 'swallow anything' (AS: 546–7). It is notable that many of the distinguished but embittered inhabitants of Galt's Gulch, the utopian community in a remote valley in Colorado that Rand presents a little over halfway through *Atlas Shrugged*, have been unable to thrive in modern academe (AS: 719).

The nature of the intelligentsia and the fate Rand thinks its members deserve are brought home to readers in a frequently cited episode in *Atlas Shrugged* in which hundreds of men, women and children die in a railway disaster when a politician insists that a train drawn by an unsuitable engine continue its journey through a long, poorly ventilated Colorado tunnel. The doomed passengers include professors of sociology, economics and philosophy who hold views Rand deplores, such as that there is no mind, logic or morality, that all human achievement is collective and that private property should be abolished. However, there are also many passengers whom anglophone readers would not normally consider 'intellectuals' but whom Russophone readers might accept as members of an intelligentsia. For example, there is a newspaper publisher who believes 'that men are evil by nature and unfit for freedom' and 'a sniveling little neurotic who wrote cheap little plays' with a 'social message'. 'These passengers', Rand observes in a concluding paragraph to the chapter which amply justifies the charge that she lacks human warmth,

> were awake; there was not a man aboard the train who did not share one or more of their ideas. As the train went into the tunnel, the flame of Wyatt's torch [from an oil-well still burning after one of Rand's admired industrialists had set it on fire in protest at government policy; DO] was the last thing they saw on earth. (*AS*: 605–7)[12]

Rand's magnum opus may therefore be classified not only as a dystopian novel but also as an anti-intelligentsia novel, insofar as she believes that a dystopia may well be a community in which 'intellectuals' hold sway. In this respect, *Atlas Shrugged* bears a resemblance to the anti-nihilist novel that was in vogue in Russia in the second half of the nineteenth century, in which members of the radical intelligentsia were portrayed as amoral, cynical and self-interested. *Troubled Seas* (1863) by Aleksei Pisemsky, *No Way Out* (1864) by Nikolai Leskov and Dostoevsky's *Devils* are notable examples of this strand of Russian prose fiction.[13] Placed in the setting of another young nation which was beginning to challenge the old European world, however, *Atlas Shrugged* functioned not so much in a conservative fashion, as a breakwater keeping back the revolutionary tide, but as a revolutionary novel preparing the ground for destruction of the old order. In this respect too, it drew on a pre-revolutionary Russian tradition.

Rand as a revolutionary novelist

The Russian anti-nihilist novel interacted with the revolutionary novel, which offered sympathetic portrayals of young men and women who started trying to put socialist ideas into effect in ways resembling those used by activists in the revolutionary movement that unfolded in Russia from the 1860s.[14] *Hard Times* (1865), by Vasilii Sleptsov, and *Andrei Kozhukhov* (1889), by a former socialist propagandist and terrorist, Sergei Kravchinsky, stand out among examples of the new revolutionary sub-genre, but here too Chernyshevsky's *What Is to Be Done?* served as a prototype. Chernyshevsky's novel is a vehicle for his social views, especially his views on the emancipation of women and the replacement of the patriarchal family with the commune or cooperative as the basic social unit. As for its plot, the novel is designed to illustrate the ethical doctrine that underpins its author's socio-political views. Lopukhov, a medical student, marries Chernyshevsky's heroine, Vera Pavlovna Rozal'skaia, who is the elder sister of a boy to whom he is a private tutor. He does this to liberate Vera from her oppressive household and to thwart her domineering mother's plan to marry her off to a wealthy man Vera detests. However, when he realizes that Vera has grown tired of him and is attracted instead to his friend and fellow medical student Kirsanov, Lopukhov disappears, pretending to have committed suicide and leaving Vera free to form a new emotional attachment. He goes to America, a country that was beginning to be perceived in Russia, and elsewhere in Europe, as a land of the future which would soon overtake the moribund 'old world' of Western Europe. Having prospered there, he returns to Russia, marries a Russian woman and renews his friendship with Kirsanov and Vera, all of whom then live happily together. The plot of *What Is to Be Done?* thus enacts rational egoism: individuals best serve their selfish interests, Chernyshevsky is arguing, by recognizing the interests of others in the larger social group.

Despite the political gulf that separates the socialist Chernyshevsky from Rand, the high priestess of capitalism, *Atlas Shrugged* does resemble *What Is to Be Done?* in many respects. As in Chernyshevsky's novel, so too in Rand's the plot is assisted by the relationships that the novel's heroine develops with some of its alpha males, and these relationships in turn facilitate the exposition of ideas that are important to the author. In *Atlas Shrugged*, there are not two but three such relationships. Rand's heroine Dagny has had a childhood friendship with Francisco, who, when Dagny is in her teens, is the first to possess her sexually. Later, as she dynamically manages the operations of her family's railway company, Dagny is powerfully attracted to Hank Rearden. Finally, she encounters John Galt, the most extraordinary of the new men in *Atlas Shrugged*, and their relationship is in due course consummated, as readers by this stage of the novel foresee without difficulty, in the first instance on sandbags on a rail track in the New York subway. Uninhibited by conventional American professions of respect for monogamy and family life (which she considered 'the glorification of mediocrity'[15]), Rand shares the belief of the Russian radical intelligentsia in the right to free love and sanctions adultery (Hank Rearden, after all, is married when he conducts his affair with Dagny).

Atlas Shrugged also resembles *What Is to Be Done?* in that Rand, like Chernyshevsky, imagines that life in her utopia will be eased by the technological improvements that will flow from her heroes' enhanced power of reasoning and capacity for empirical thinking. In both novels, certain buildings symbolize this happy advance. Chernyshevsky's Vera Pavlovna, in the last of four allegorical dreams which chart her journey from a fusty underground to a radiant world blessed by rational decision-making and scientific progress, sees a building which brings to mind the Crystal Palace, that monument to Victorian technological achievement which housed the Great Exhibition of 1851 in London.[16] In Rand's fiction too, we find buildings which have emblematic significance. In *The Fountainhead*, Roark expresses his genius and soaring imagination through his architectural work, especially the construction of skyscrapers in New York. In *Atlas Shrugged*, Rand again admires the skyline of 'the greatest city in the world' (*AS*: 443), which her heroes see as both their own creation and their natural habitat (*AS*: 1138). From her vantage point as a resident of the city while it remains in its dystopian pre-revolutionary state, Dagny 'looked at the great skyscrapers in the distance. [...] Once, they had been a promise, and from the midst of the stagnant sloth around her she had looked to them for proof that another kind of men existed' (*AS*: 905). Another such emblematic building is located in Galt's Gulch. This is the small, austere block with a door consisting of a single sheet of stainless steel which houses the generator Galt has invented to convert static energy into kinetic power. This 'unobtrusive little structure' is in fact a prodigious feat of nano-technology (*AS*: 729–33). In both *What Is to Be Done?* and *Atlas Shrugged*, moreover, a metallurgical discovery symbolizes the achievement of the inhabitants of the author's brave new world. In the ideal community on the banks of the river Oka of which Vera Pavlovna dreams in Chernyshevsky's novel, the metal that will transform human lives is aluminium, recently introduced to the public at the Paris Exhibition of 1855 and remarkable for its lightness.[17] In Rand's fictional America, it is Rearden Metal, which is exceptionally light and strong.

Chernyshevsky's novel provided inspiration and guidance for that wing of the Russian intelligentsia which had no confidence in liberals' plans for gradual, evolutionary change but began instead to hatch more radical plans that they hoped would ultimately lead to revolution. Its most exemplary character, from the point of view of would-be revolutionaries, is Rakhmetov, who occupies centre stage quite briefly a little over halfway through *What Is to Be Done?* Just as Lopukhov and Kirsanov, who are themselves people of a new type, look up to Rakhmetov, so Rand's other positive heroes in *Atlas Shrugged* accept that Galt is *primus inter pares*. Like Rakhmetov, Galt possesses all the qualities his creator believes a successful revolutionary will need. Rand even seems to agree with Chernyshevsky on what these qualities are. Both authors envisage supermen who have great physical resilience and can function for days on end without sleep if occupied with matters they consider important (*AS*: 88). Rakhmetov has steeled himself physically and mentally to withstand hardship and even torture through his high-protein diet, his regime of physical labour and exercise, and his habit of lying on a bed of nails.[18] Similarly, Galt, when he is actually tortured by his enemies near the end of the novel, is able by virtue of his physical and mental strength to bear the ordeal and even destroy the morale of his torturers by pointing out to them the technical reason why the instrument of torture they are using keeps breaking down (AS: 1139–46). Most importantly, both Rakhmetov and Galt have attained a new philosophical understanding of the error of the way in which humans have hitherto lived. Consequently, they have found the key (rational egoism, though Chernyshevsky and Rand understand the concept differently, as we shall see) to the establishment of a new way of living.

Chernyshevsky's *What Is to Be Done?* was published at a time of intellectual revolt, social unrest and anxiety about the possibility of revolutionary upheaval in Russia after the abolition of serfdom in 1861. In Leninist terminology, the conditions of the years 1859–61 in Russia amounted to a 'revolutionary situation', that is to say a crisis in which the ruling class could not continue to govern as they had before and the governed were not prepared to go on living as they had previously.[19] The economic and political dysfunction that Rand describes from the opening page of *Atlas Shrugged* also presents a revolutionary situation, and Rand in effect asks the same question as Chernyshevsky (and forty years later, Lenin) about what is to be done in these circumstances. Like them, she answers that a revolution must indeed be carried out. (Chernyshevsky, writing under tsarist censorship, could only hint at this outcome.) Like Lenin, Rand has in mind action by a highly organized, disciplined, far-sighted minority with an advanced philosophical and political consciousness. However, revolutions are not necessarily events that bring socialists to power, and Rand's version of the phenomenon would be an antithesis of the communist revolution executed in her homeland in 1917.

The members of Rand's vanguard propose to carry out their revolution by using against the modern American government one of the weapons employed by the European labour movement that had begun to develop in the nineteenth century, namely strike action. (In fact, *The Strike* was the working title of Rand's novel almost until she finished it.[20]) By persuading those energetic individuals who drive the economy to withdraw their support for the political regime and the common run of humans who sanction it, Galt intends to 'stop the motor of the world' (AS: 671). The strike he leads brings about the economic and political collapse of the United States. For Rand's heroes, this is a welcome outcome, because the modern American nation has elevated the public good above the interests of the inventor and the successful capitalist entrepreneur, deviating from the natural path taken by its eighteenth-century founders and nineteenth-century pioneers.

In view of the widespread admiration of Rand's ideas, it seems important to underline the fact that Rand's revolutionaries know very well what the consequences of their action, or rather inaction, will be. There will be 'plain, open, blind, arbitrary, bloodshedding violence, running amuck, hitting anything and anyone at random' and 'the senseless, unpredictable dangers of a world falling apart', explains the successful banker 'Midas' Mulligan, who had purchased the land in Galt's Gulch on which the revolutionaries' utopian community was set up. 'Plane crashes, oil tank explosions, blast-furnace break-outs, high-tension wire electrocutions, subway cave-ins and trestle collapses' – Rand has Mulligan list the likely results of their strike, relishing both the anticipated mayhem and her own technological know-how. When the railway lines are cut, New York will starve in two days, but before that happens, Mulligan warns, 'they'll go through the whole of the agony – through the shrinking, the shortages, the hunger riots, the stampeding violence in the midst of the growing stillness' (AS: 804–6). Shortly after Mulligan has made these dire predictions, failure to deliver a sufficient number of freight wagons to transport the vital crop of wheat from Minnesota results in the rotting of the harvested grain and the outbreak of serious social unrest (AS: 936–43). The work of revolutionary destruction is complete when, in the closing pages of the novel, Francisco, Ragnar, Rearden and Dagny fly with Galt, whom they have just freed from the torture-chamber in the State Science Institute, over New York. Suddenly, this city, the hub of world civilization in Rand's mental landscape, is plunged into darkness at the moment when the population is desperately trying to flee and the power stations which keep it functioning fail (AS: 1158).

Rand's positive heroes look with equanimity on these consequences of their actions. This is partly because those who perish are expendable and in some sense deserving of their fate, inasmuch as they have never chosen to use their minds and engage in what Rand would regard as intelligent, logical thought. Her heroes' sangfroid is also due to their Machiavellian or Jesuitical conviction that their end is so important that it is legitimate to use any means to achieve it. In this regard, they have an affinity with those Russian revolutionaries, including Lenin, who were unfastidious in their choice of methods. Rand's positive heroes, it is true, seem for a while to have some qualms about Ragnar's piracy (*AS*: 575), but none makes any attempt to thwart it. Indeed, this piracy is of critical importance to their revolutionary enterprise. It destroys the commercial traffic and supplies of their enemies and enables them to accumulate gold, the guarantee of the stable currency they prize. It is also a terrorist tactic intended to inspire awe: anyone who attempts independently to produce Rearden Metal, Ragnar assures Rearden, will 'find his furnaces blown up, his machinery blasted, his shipments wrecked, his plant set on fire' (*AS*: 581). Rand's heroes are no more squeamish than the Bolsheviks about the means they use, or threaten to use, to accomplish their aims.

The ultimate aims of revolutionaries, of course, are to establish an ideal order of their own imagining, ensure its security and, if possible, universalize it. Their more immediate aim, though, is to overthrow the old order. This latter task requires 'destroyers' in the mould of the 'nihilists' imagined by Russian thinkers and writers of the 1860s. Pisarev, the most prominent representative of this type, thought it necessary to demolish the aesthetic, moral and social assumptions on which the present order was based and to replace them with empirically tested, 'scientific' deductions before the world could be reconstructed as a place fit for humans of the modern age. The literary prototype for such a nihilist is Bazarov in Turgenev's novel *Fathers and Children*, for whom the first step is 'to clear space' in preparation for future building.[21]

The type of destroyer exemplified by Pisarev and Bazarov is much feared by certain characters in *Atlas Shrugged* until they understand his true function as the most effective warrior against the collectivist establishment that is to blame for America's degeneration. Dagny's assistant Willers, for example, muses on the 'ruthless creature moved by some inconceivable purpose' who is 'draining the brains of the world' (*AS*: 439). He is echoing the words of Dagny herself, who anxiously asks Francisco whether there is 'actually a destroyer loose in the world' (*AS*: 637). Indeed, there is, but Dagny should not fear him, as she eventually realizes after she has encountered Galt and he has begun to inculcate proper revolutionary consciousness in her. By the novel's final page, when parts of the country are in a state of civil war, the initial stage of the mission of Rand's heroes has been completed. 'The road is cleared', Galt proclaims in his last utterance in *Atlas Shrugged*, repeating the image that has been used, by Rand and by Russian nihilists before her, real and literary, to evoke revolution (*AS*: 1168). The work of reconstruction can now begin.

Thus, the revolution that Rand's conspirators plan and bring about and the actions that lead up to it have features familiar from Russian and other revolutionary histories. These features include the effectiveness of crippling industrial action, tensions and bitter animosities within the nation, a single-minded determination on the part of the revolutionaries to achieve their ends (which makes them indifferent to the infliction of heavy casualties on opponents and neutrals) and subjection of the country to an economic and political crisis that leads to the breakdown of the old order. This destructive phase must take place before society can be rebuilt in a way that the victors in the struggle will consider just. At the same time, the revolution executed by the positive heroes of *Atlas Shrugged* is a reversal of the sort of revolutions brought about in the twentieth century (for example, in Russia, China, North Vietnam, Cuba and even, as Rand sees it, early post-war Britain[22]) by socialists of one hue or another. Rand's revolution will not bring about a society fashioned in accordance with the Marxian slogan 'From each according to his ability, to each according to his need' (*AS*: 323, 661). Quite the reverse: it will restore individualism and capitalism, as Rand makes clear in the novel's last sentence, in which Galt 'raised his hand and over the desolate earth [...] traced in space the sign of the dollar' (*AS*: 1168).

In framing her programme of revolutionary action, Rand consistently subverts the concepts and vocabulary of Marxism, the version of socialist doctrine expounded in its most compelling popular form in the *Manifesto of the Communist Party* written by Marx and Engels in 1848. In the 'Manifesto of Individualism' she wrote in

1941, in which she celebrated capitalism as 'the noblest, cleanest and most idealistic system of all', she rebuffed the exhortation addressed by Marx and Engels to working men of all countries to unite with a slogan of her own (albeit an oxymoronic one), 'Individualists of the World Unite!'[23] In *Atlas Shrugged*, her heroes continue the attempt to turn Marxism inside out. Whereas it is proletarians, according to Marx and Engels, who are in chains and inhumanly exploited, for Galt and Rearden it is industrialists who are chained and in need of liberation (*AS*: 933, 1039). Whereas a Marxist will argue that those who control the means of production expropriate the commodities produced by proletarians and realize their value, Rand's Ragnar believes that the value of goods that have been produced thanks only to the initiative of a small number of superior humans has been expropriated by undeserving labourers and 'looters' (*AS*: 578–9). Rand has thus identified new victims of injustice and reversed the supposed 'pattern of "exploitation"' that Marxists have instilled in the consciousness of millions. The country's wealthiest and most energetic entrepreneurs are transformed, in her mirror-image of Marxism, into unappreciated, poorly remunerated, pitiable victims of a greedy mass of second-rate humans.

Rand's grievance about the victimization of 'the oppressed, the disinherited, the exploited' (*AS*: 746) – a grievance she repeated in a lecture on 'America's persecuted minority: big business', published in 1962[24] – goes beyond a sense of economic injustice. It takes on an ontological dimension when Galt presents the plight of Rand's heroes as the exclusion of the chosen. The listeners whom he berates in his broadcast to the nation have sought 'to exile from the human race the hero, the thinker, the producer, the inventor, the strong, the purposeful, the pure' (*AS*: 1050). Rand herself, externalizing Dagny's thoughts, even presents those whom she considers heroic beings as martyrs, like the property developers and architects who had expressed the values she admires by building the skyscrapers of Manhattan. In America's new dystopian age, these buildings seemed like 'tombstones, slender obelisks soaring in memory of the men who had been destroyed for having created them, […] the frozen shape of the silent cry that reward of achievement was martyrdom' (*AS*: 905). As men who never compromise and are prepared to die for a subversive idea, Rand's heroes have something in common with Russia's numerous revolutionary terrorists (women, as well as men, incidentally), who from the mid-1870s to the early 1900s often explicitly presented themselves as martyrs and were widely perceived as such.

Rand and the Socialist Realist novel

Insofar as Rand's execution of a revolutionary novel amounts to an attempt to turn Marxism inside out, *Atlas Shrugged* may also be seen as a subversion of the Socialist Realist prose fiction produced in the first two decades of Soviet power. Characterized as 'a sort of parable for the working-out of Marxism-Leninism in history', the early Socialist Realist novel dealt primarily with the Civil War that followed the October Revolution or the industrialization of the USSR after that war.[25] The literary movement formally known from the early 1930s as 'Socialist Realism' had roots in the view of art propounded by Chernyshevsky, Dobroliubov, Pisarev and other radical critics of the 1860s and drew on aspects of the late-nineteenth-century Russian revolutionary novel. Socialist Realist works that came to be regarded as canonical texts in the Soviet Union started to appear in the early 1920s, while Rand still lived in her Russian homeland and as the Bolsheviks began to exercise control over cultural production. Writers deemed to be Socialist Realists found inspiration in the work of major novelists of the past, foreign as well as Russian, who were thought to have been attuned to the consciousness of the common people and progressive in their time, such as Balzac, Dickens and Émile Zola, and, in Russia, Tolstoy and Gorky.[26] They were expected to display 'party-mindedness' (*partiinost'*) and to convey a positive, optimistic message. It was their duty to promote the policies of the Communist Party by correctly interpreting the party's ideology (which was liable to shift suddenly as circumstances changed) and to assure readers that the party would eventually fulfil all its goals.

Of course, Rand, the champion of individualism and capitalism, stood in the opposite ideological camp from supporters of Bolshevism, who used Marxist-Leninist ideology to underpin a highly centralized and increasingly authoritarian state which managed a planned economy. Nonetheless, typical features of novels in the Socialist Realist canon are replicated in *The Fountainhead* and *Atlas Shrugged*, sometimes with Rand's characteristic inversions of concepts she wished to challenge. They may have found their way into her fiction because Rand was directly familiar with many of the texts in question (some of which were translated and published abroad, especially in America, quite soon after they appeared in the USSR) or simply because she was familiar with such features in the Russian antecedents of the Socialist Realist novel.

Some of these replicated features concern the positive literary hero. Socialist Realist heroes, after all, are capable, as Rand's would be, of dedicating their life to the realization of their goal and pursue that goal with a combination of will, determination and self-discipline. A prime example is Pavel Korchagin, the hero of Nikolai Ostrovsky's *How Steel Was Tempered* (completed and first published in 1932–4). Korchagin devotes himself to the Bolshevik cause, shuns emotional relationships which might weaken his political resolve and subdues human weaknesses that he recognizes in himself, such as smoking and swearing (hence the reference to tempering steel in Ostrovsky's title).[27] Another attribute of exemplary characters in Socialist Realist novels is philosophical and political consciousness (*soznatel'nost'*, in formal Socialist Realist parlance). Thus, in Dmitrii Furmanov's *Chapaev* (1923), whose eponymous central character is a legendary commander in the Civil War, the author's alter ego, Fedor Klychkov, has the task of instilling into this spontaneous, semi-literate peasant soldier the ideological awareness that will maximize his effectiveness in the service of the Bolsheviks.[28] Rand's principal heroes (Galt, Francisco and Ragnar in *Atlas Shrugged*) deplore the notion of the public good and feel none of the sense of duty that motivates Korchagin or Klychkov. And yet, they too see it as their role to inspire and raise the awareness of others (most notably Dagny and Hank Rearden) who are temperamentally sympathetic to their goals but as yet lack *soznatel'nost'*. They also regard themselves as potential martyrs, like many a hero or heroine of Socialist Realist fiction, such as the eponymous mother of Gorky's inspirational novel *The Mother* (1907), which charts the radicalization and martyrdom of a pious widow whose son is arrested for revolutionary activity.[29]

Rand's novels also resemble classic Socialist Realist texts in that they describe epic struggles in which ideologically pure heroes triumph because of their determination in the face of apparently overwhelming odds. The formidable adversaries whom Socialist Realist heroes have to overcome include the White Army led by Admiral Kolchak in the Civil War (as in *Chapaev*) and political foes such as Trotskyites and saboteurs (as in Fedor Gladkov's *Energy* (1932–8)). Rand's heroes have to show similar resolve in order to achieve personal success in a hostile professional environment, in Roark's case, or to bring about a far-reaching socio-economic and political transformation, in the case of Galt and his co-revolutionaries. Or again, Socialist Realist heroes may meet resistance from dangerous class enemies of bourgeois or narrow bureaucratic mindset, who crop up, for instance, as opponents of an effective cooperative unit of workers in Gladkov's novella *The Oath* (1944).[30] Such moaners, who stand in the way of self-willed positive heroes, seem in retrospect to be precursors of Rand's counter-revolutionary whiners, snivellers and moochers, who themselves will become the 'doomsters and gloomsters', 'naysayers', and 'remoaners' berated by the modern British right.

Rand is also inspired, like the authors of the Socialist Realist production novel, by the story of breakneck industrialization. The best-known prototype of such a novel is Gladkov's *Cement* (1925), in which the hero, Gleb Chumalov, returns to his hometown after the Civil War and sets about rebuilding the ruined factory where he had previously worked. Later, in *Energy*, Gladkov chronicled the construction of a hydro-electric power station during the first five-year plan, offering another example of the new Soviet type of positive hero, Vatagin, the director of a gigantic industrial project.[31] Gladkov, of course, is concerned with the achievements that are supposed to result from collective work in communist society. By contrast, industrial progress in Rand's fictional world springs from the genius and energy of private individuals who are motivated by a quest for wealth and personal self-realization. *Atlas Shrugged* is nonetheless reminiscent of the early Soviet industrial novel in certain respects.[32] Rand too is interested in the technological achievement made possible by the rapid advance of scientific knowledge in an increasingly secular world. Insofar as she finds poetry anywhere, it is in furnaces, coke ovens, conveyor belts, railway track, metal mills, 'snatches of red above black funnels, long coils of steam, the webbed diagonals of cranes and bridges', and in 'roving streamers of flame, with the ladles of molten metal sailing through space on delicate cables' (*AS*: 215, 932). She too expresses wonderment at feats of engineering, exemplified in *Atlas Shrugged* by the maiden journey of a Taggart train travelling through Wyoming and Colorado at a hundred miles an hour on track made of Rearden Metal and over a bridge of the same alloy suspended over an abyss.

Rand's very purpose as a novelist, finally, is foreshadowed in early Soviet literary discourse. She is the author of works which, like the Soviet novel, perform 'a totally different function from the one the novel performs in the West'. This difference in function gives rise to a different kind of text, to which the methods of evaluation customarily used by Western critics and scholars are not applicable.[33] Like a good Socialist Realist, Rand creates characters who belong to a type considered by the author as either admirable or reprehensible and produces novels which have ideological content, or *ideinost'*, another key attribute of Socialist Realist literature. Like a communist ideologue, she tries to convey a straightforward message and treats ideas as right or wrong. Her conception of the writer's task resembles that of Socialist Realists, who, despite their commitment to matter-of-fact Realism, were also prone to revolutionary Romanticism, idealizing warriors who battled for what ought to be.[34] She too was a zealous cultural propagandist, as we see from a set of commandments to the Motion Picture Alliance for the Preservation of American Ideals that she published in a 'Screen Guide for Americans' in 1947, as McCarthyism was gathering pace.[35] It is therefore apt to use the term 'Capitalist Realism' to describe Rand's fiction,[36] for it is a counter-weight to, but also has much in common with, the Socialist Realism that was being promoted in the Soviet Union from around the time Rand left it.

CHAPTER 4
ETHICAL, METAPHYSICAL AND EPISTEMOLOGICAL QUESTIONS

Altruism is bad and egoism is good

Conducting a reappraisal of values in the early 1860s in the light of Western ideas that Russia had recently encountered, Chernyshevsky and Dostoevsky debated aesthetics, materialism (in the philosophical sense that matter is the only or the fundamental reality), human nature, the effect of social and physiological factors on an individual's behaviour, and political ideas. They approached these subjects from an atheistic socialist and a Christian conservative standpoint respectively.[1] At the very centre of their outlooks were ethical doctrines which seem at first sight to be diametrically opposed to one another but which in fact attach equal importance to harmonious human association.

In his *Winter Notes on Summer Impressions* (1863), a work written apropos of his first trip to Western Europe in 1862, Dostoevsky argued that individuals found their highest fulfilment in voluntary self-sacrifice for the benefit of others, without the slightest regard for their own self-interest – in other words, by following Christ's example.[2] Chernyshevsky, on the other hand, put forward a utilitarian doctrine, according to which humans did act in their own interest, seeking pleasure and avoiding pain. And yet, Chernyshevsky's rational egoism was designed, like the plot of his novel *What Is to Be Done?*, to persuade readers that the personal interests they inevitably pursue are best served if they act in ways that benefit the larger community. Being rational creatures, Chernyshevsky believed, humans could be made to understand that it was to their advantage to behave in this cooperative way. In other words, Chernyshevsky's rational egoism was in truth also conceived as a species of altruism, a guarantee of the preservation of a sense of brotherhood in a post-Christian world.

Rand, like Chernyshevsky, preached a form of egoism, but a form in which the poles of conventional morality were unashamedly reversed. In her moral universe, what had previously been considered fair was foul and foul was fair. The Christian commandment that we love our neighbour as ourselves and the socialist appeal to secular brotherhood were equally objectionable to her on the grounds that they both prioritize the interests of the collective over those of the self. A critique of altruism, the principle of acting or living for others, is the bedrock of both her major novels.

In *The Fountainhead*, Rand pursues her goal by associating the sin she wishes to eradicate with her anti-hero Toohey, who is 'a sort of one-man holding company of altruism' (*F*: 310). Disparaging individualism and speaking of the private ego as a 'miser's hole', Toohey claims to be searching for 'the sense of universal equality, the great peace of brotherhood, a new world' in which humans should strive to merge their individual spirits 'with the vast collective spirit of mankind' (*F*: 300, 307). This apparently selfless quest leads him logically to socialism, which he had discovered at the age of sixteen (*F*: 306). It turns out, though, that Toohey conceives of altruism merely as a concept with which power-hungry men like himself have managed in all societies to enslave lesser beings. All great systems of ethics, he explains, as his true character is revealed towards the end of the novel, have used the leitmotif of 'sacrifice, renunciation, self-denial' to tie happiness to guilt, thereby seizing humankind 'by the throat' (*F*: 666). Rand also attacks altruists more directly in *The Fountainhead* through her mouthpiece Roark, who argues ingeniously in his court-room speech that those who 'have been taught that their first concern is to relieve the suffering of others' must perversely wish to see others suffer so that they can display this concern (*F*: 713).

In *Atlas Shrugged*, Rand has most of her major positive characters explicitly repeat her critique of altruism in much the same terms she had used in *The Fountainhead*. When Dagny hears someone insisting that people should be motivated 'not by personal gain, but by love for their brothers', a cold, implacable inner voice advises her to pay close attention, for 'it is not often that one can see pure evil' (*AS*: 323). Through Galt, Rand again deplores both the varieties of altruism, religious and secular (both a Dostoevskian and a Chernyshevskian variety, we could say), that she has identified. 'No matter how loudly they posture in the roles of irreconcilable antagonists', Galt declares in his broadcast to the American people, the two types of altruist have similar moral codes and aims: 'in matter – the enslavement of man's body, in spirit – the destruction of his mind' (*AS*: 1027). Once more, altruism is condemned on the grounds that it burdens people with a sense of responsibility for all their fellows, causes a sense of guilt and enables mediocrities to keep the world's most original, independent spirits in check. It is a punitive 'system of thought', applied 'on a world scale', which has produced nothing less, Francisco omnisciently explains, than the greatest moral crisis the world has ever faced (*AS*: 61, 619).

It is probable that Rand was personally unable to believe, as Dostoevsky did, that there are humans who are prepared willingly, indeed lovingly, to suppress their own interests for the sake of others and even to sacrifice their lives for fellow beings. Or, to put the matter in the utilitarian terms preferred by Chernyshevsky, the notion that human individuals could derive personal pleasure from acting in the interests of others made no sense to her. Be that as it may, her mission was to sweep away for ever the altruists' moral code, which she considered 'irrational',[3] and to replace it with its antithesis. Those who oppose her heroes are given an 'ultimatum', which is couched, incidentally, in terms that underline the materialistic, futuristic nature of the utopia towards which Rand wishes to guide her readers. 'If you desire ever again to live in an *industrial* society' (my italics; DO), Galt warns the failing American nation, then 'it will be on *our* moral terms' (*AS*: 1024; Rand's italics). These terms, it turns out in both *The Fountainhead* and *Atlas Shrugged*, are unashamedly egoistic. Man, Galt tells the nation, 'exists for his own sake, and the achievement of his own happiness is his highest moral purpose' (*AS*: 1014). This hard-and-fast moral law is carved in granite above the stainless-steel door of the structure Galt has built in his utopian community to house his generator and serves as an oath required of those who wish to enter this community: 'I swear by my life and my love of it that I will never live for the sake of another man, nor ask another man to live for mine' (AS: 731).[4]

Atlas Shrugged is thus a celebration of the striving of the ego to realize itself through complete control over whatever possessions the individual can acquire and through exercise of the independent mind with which humans are endowed, although few seem capable of using it. Nor is egoism the only Christian vice that Rand re-evaluates. From the point of view of the self-loving ego, the cardinal Christian sin of pride is not 'the worst of all sins', as James Taggart believes it to be (AS: 264). In fact, it is not a sin at all, in Galt's opinion, but 'the sum of all virtues'. Humans should discard instead 'the protective rags' of humility, another Randian vice, like altruism, which had mistakenly been regarded by Christians as a virtue (AS: 1059).

Many characters in her novels whom Rand portrays in an unfavourable light (especially members of the families of her heroes or heroines) perceive her paragons as 'selfish', 'unyielding', 'intractable', 'unbearably conceited' and even 'inhuman' (AS: 37, 51, 301, 466). Understandable as many readers will consider such reactions, Rand the mature author – like Alisa the child who was often chided by her mother – saw no reason why her heroes should be reproached for displaying attitudes which made others consider them difficult. Pushing her defence of egoism to an extreme, she seems oblivious of the sort of moral or emotional obstacles – concern for others, compassion or the desire to seek common ground or behave in a conciliatory way – that might prevent people from pursuing their personal goals as ruthlessly as they could. If empathy can be defined as the 'ability to share someone else's feelings or experiences by imagining what it would be like to be in that person's situation',[5] then Rand lacked it or saw no need for it. The inability or refusal of her heroes to concede that other humans may sincerely experience altruistic impulses; their imperviousness to a sense of guilt; their self-absorption and unapologetic, relentless pursuit of their personal interest: these characteristics tend to place Rand's favourite characters in a marginal band on the spectrum of social behaviour, a band accommodating those whom psychologists classify as 'asocial' or 'antisocial'. She is the cold, stony advocate of self-interest, the poet of the sociopath.

Ordinary and extraordinary members of the human race

The debate in the Russian intelligentsia about dystopias and utopias, revolution and morality, of which Rand's writings are on one level a continuation, included attempts to identify categories of people who might be capable of initiating and directing the transformations deemed necessary or whose natures would make it possible or impossible for them to settle into the new kinds of societies that were being imagined.

In 'Bazarov' (1862), an essay that Pisarev wrote apropos of Turgenev's *Fathers and Children*, for example, human beings were divided into three categories (*razriady*). First, there is the ordinary mass of humans who live 'according to the established norm', neither making discoveries nor committing crimes. Second, there are more intelligent individuals who cannot easily come to terms with everything that the mass accepts but who are not capable of taking their rebellion beyond a theoretical stage. Third, there are individuals who can 'mark themselves off' from the mass 'by their acts, habits and whole way of life', achieving 'full self-liberation, full individuality (*osobnost'*) and independence'.[6] Lest he fall foul of the censors who redacted every Russian publication in his day, Pisarev uses Aesopian language here, but his more astute readers would easily have construed his remarks about people who could fully liberate themselves as praise for potential revolutionaries.

Individuals in Pisarev's highest category are obviously on a par with the young socialists and rational egoists whom Chernyshevsky imagines in *What Is to Be Done?* Chernyshevsky may be less interested than Pisarev in defining the ordinary mass of humans, but he pays special attention to the most 'extraordinary' representatives of his admirable 'new people'. These belong to the 'breed' exemplified in his novel by Rakhmetov, people so rare that Chernyshevsky's narrator has met only eight of them in his life. The Rakhmetovs of the world are 'the flower of the best people, the movers among the movers, the salt of the salt of the earth'.[7]

Dostoevsky took up Chernyshevsky's essentially binary classification in *Crime and Punishment*, where he had his murderer,

Raskol'nikov, outline his thoughts on the categories (*razriady* again) into which humans could be divided. In his first, lower category, Raskol'nikov places 'ordinary' conservative, orderly people whose functions in life are to propagate their own kind and to obey. In his higher category, he places 'extraordinary' individuals who consider themselves entitled to step over existing legal or moral boundaries in order to utter some '*new word*'. These people 'move the world and lead it towards a goal'. That goal, it is hinted, might be the building of a New Jerusalem, an ideal in which Raskol'nikov says he believes. Dostoevsky's list of examples of such exceptional people included a prophet (Mohammed), an empire-builder (Napoleon), ancient law-givers (Lycurgus of Sparta and Solon of Athens) and natural scientists (the astronomer Johannes Kepler and the mathematician and physicist Isaac Newton).[8]

In Rand's fictional universe, humans are divided into ordinary and extraordinary beings in much the same way that they are by Chernyshevsky and by Raskol'nikov in Dostoevsky's *Crime and Punishment*, although Rand would have agreed with Raskol'nikov that there was an infinite number of possible sub-divisions of people within each category.[9] She also admits of the possibility, like Pisarev, that there are certain people who find their society unsatisfactory but are not capable of decisively breaking with it. These are people, as Francisco helpfully explains in *Atlas Shrugged*, who cannot equal the power of Rearden's mind or invent new metals that revolutionize industrial production but work just as hard, live by their own effort and silently thank superior men such as Rearden who give them more than they themselves can give the world. Dagny's loyal assistant Eddie Willers is identified by Francisco as a person of this middling kind. His usefulness to the novel's heroes is not in doubt, but he is not fit to enter the utopia they are constructing, as Rand makes clear when, in the last chapter of the novel, she brutally abandons him by a broken-down train in the Arizona desert, like the captain of a stricken vessel going down with his ship (*AS*: 453, 1160–7). The existence of such doubters in the status quo does not fundamentally alter the larger picture in Rand's universe, in which there is a natural schism between two human categories of the sort that Raskol'nikov had defined.

We have a foretaste of what Rand thinks of the lower category when her mouthpiece in *We the Living*, Kira Argounova, expresses her view of the popular masses who were making their presence felt in revolutionary Russia (*WL*: 42). What are they, she asks her communist lover Andrei, 'but millions of dull, shrivelled stagnant souls that have no thoughts of their own, no dreams of their own, no will of their own, who eat and sleep and chew helplessly the words others put into their brains?' Men are not equal in ability, Kira complains, and should not be treated as if they were. Besides, Kira loathes most of them (*WL*: 74).

In her mature novels, Rand's contempt for 'average humanity' or the 'common herd' is similarly unbounded.[10] People of this ordinary sort make up what Akston in *Atlas Shrugged* calls a 'gibbering swamp of mediocrity' (*AS*: 789). They span a broad social, economic and intellectual range from down-and-out 'bums' and people who work in menial jobs, such as janitors and filing clerks, to officials who are 'looters', educated professionals such as conventional architects, 'humanitarians' and members of the intelligentsia who hold views that Rand considers pernicious. These 'second-raters' from across the social spectrum are castigated on account of their allegedly exploitative and manipulative altruistic ethics, their appeals to public interest and their envious censure of the self-interested wealthy entrepreneur. In moral terms, they all have a certain likeness to one another inasmuch as they have a sense of entitlement but lack talent and are idle and parasitic. They are 'second-handers' or 'hitchhikers', as Roark in *The Fountainhead* and Francisco in *Atlas Shrugged* respectively like to call them (*F*: 715, *AS*: 418).[11] That is to say, they feed off the genius of more creative humans in order to make a mark in the world. In the first of these novels, the most egregious 'second-hander' is the architect Peter Keating, who repeatedly uses Roark's designs to advance his own career and reputation. In the second, it is James Taggart, who garners the financial profit and reputational credit that flow from his sister's tireless management of the operations of the family railway company. All of them, Francisco complains, are 'whining rotters who never rouse themselves to any effort, who do not possess the ability of a filing clerk, but demand the income of a company president' (*AS*: 453).

Such people have managed to live for millennia at the expense of the elite in whatever society they happen to inhabit because they have calculated that the productive few will assume any burden 'in order to work and produce', even though they are not properly recognized or rewarded for their creativity (*AS*: 619). Rand really does suspect, it seems, that an age-old, universal conspiracy is in operation.

To the ordinary human beings whom she places in this abhorrent inferior category of humankind, Rand starkly contrasts her extraordinary exemplary characters. Of these, only a few – Roark in *The Fountainhead*; Galt, Francisco and Hank Rearden in *Atlas Shrugged* – have already reached full understanding of their powers and how to use them when we first meet them. These are 'giants of productive energy', the 'creators', who have been 'denied, opposed, persecuted, exploited' but have nonetheless invented things and 'carried all humanity along' (*F*: 453, 715). They belong to the same breed as those special people whom Chernyshevsky had called the 'salt of the salt of the earth'. Other positive characters, such as Dagny Taggart, experience an epiphany as a result of their exposure to them.

Irrefutable evidence of Rand's unacknowledged debt to Dostoevsky's Raskol'nikov for her classification of humankind and her characterization of her heroes is to be found towards the end of *The Fountainhead*, when she has her newspaper owner, Gail Wynand, spring to Roark's defence. Wynand's paper publishes a series of articles on famous trials of innocent men who 'had been convicted by the majority prejudice of the moment' and 'martyred by society', in other words exceptional individuals like Roark who heroically stand alone and defy lesser, rule-bound humans. Although the list of extraordinary people extolled in Wynand's series is shorter than Raskol'nikov's and has a narrower focus (no prophet or law-giver, for instance, is named in it), in essence Rand follows Raskol'nikov's model, focusing on thinkers and scientists (Socrates, Galileo and Pasteur) who have broken the mould by fearlessly uttering some new word (*F*: 654).

Lacking any sense of obligation to others, or guilt for their selfishness, or respect for any external moral restraint, Rand's heroes (especially her heroes in *Atlas Shrugged*) also resemble Dostoevskian characters, and their successor, the Nietzschean *Übermensch*, in that they are conceived as man-gods. In a world in which people no longer believe in God or immortality, they share the assumption to which Ivan Karamazov had given currency in Dostoevsky's last novel that 'all is permitted' to them.[12] They gain enormous power as a result and may consequently overawe others. Dagny, for example, feels so overwhelmed when she first encounters Galt in person that she loses her sense of herself as a separate entity: 'she was not a person, only a function, the function of seeing him, and the sight was its own meaning and purpose, with no further end to reach' (*AS*: 733).

In fact, Rand's most extraordinary heroes are portrayed as demigods. In both *The Fountainhead* and *Atlas Shrugged*, and also in her earlier novella *Anthem*, Rand likens her paragon to Prometheus, the Titan who steals fire from Zeus and gives it to humans. For this daring rebellion, according to the ancient Greek myth, Zeus had punished Prometheus by chaining him to a rock, where a vulture fed each day on his liver, which was restored during each succeeding night. In *Anthem*, Rand's hero Equality 7-2521 renames himself Prometheus after he has freed himself from the collectivist 'City' which suppresses all human individuality. In *The Fountainhead*, Roark invokes Prometheus as one of those heroic beings who have bequeathed to humanity some beneficial new idea but have been condemned to suffer for their temerity, because they have been regarded as transgressors who have ventured into 'forbidden territory' (*F*: 710). In *Atlas Shrugged*, finally, Francisco explains to Dagny that

> John Galt is Prometheus who changed his mind. After centuries of being torn by vultures in payment for having brought to men the fire of the gods, he broke his chains and he withdrew his fire – until the day when men withdraw their vultures. (*AS*: 517)

The association of Randian superheroes with a Titan affirms their status as rule-breakers and benefactors of humanity who discover new knowledge and bring about the improvements in human life that ordinary mortals unashamedly enjoy. Nor is Prometheus the only demigod of whom Rand's modern heroes think when they decide on what terms they are prepared to work, create and produce. What would happen, the title of Rand's magnum opus invites readers to consider, if Atlas, the Titan god of endurance who has stoically borne the world on his shoulders, were suddenly to make a gesture of indifference? The world would of course collapse, as indeed it does when Galt withdraws his superhuman support.

Dualism and monism, determinism, reason and volition

Rand took great pains to construct what she considered a comprehensive and highly original philosophical foundation for the world-outlook of her extraordinary new humans. For almost two years, sustained by daily doses of a pill containing an amphetamine and a barbiturate of which she was a long-term user,[13] she laboured over the chapter 'This Is John Galt Speaking', which she conceived as the intellectual climax of *Atlas Shrugged*. Boldly venturing into metaphysics, epistemology, politics and economics, as well as ethics, Galt claims to complete the thought of Aristotle, whose 'formula defining the concept of existence and the rule of all knowledge', namely 'A is A. A thing is itself', had never been properly understood until he, Galt (and by extension his creator), explained its true meaning (*AS*: 1016). In Galt's monologue, and in many other passages in the novel, Rand tries to complete, systematize and bolster the philosophical credibility of the world-view that underpins the conduct of her superheroes and legitimizes their pursuit of their own ends. Most of the propositions she sets out, many of which had been rehearsed in *The Fountainhead*, are reminiscent of statements in the writings of pre-revolutionary Russian thinkers and writers. She draws to a considerable extent on propositions widely shared by radical thinkers but also baulks at the deterministic ideas they often propounded, as did some radical thinkers themselves, from Chernyshevsky to Lenin, when those ideas conflicted with their wish to give history a push.

Firstly, Rand actually follows Chernyshevsky and many other pre-revolutionary Russian radicals in rejecting the notion of dualism, according to which humans have both physical and spiritual being. The intellectual opponents of Rand's heroes 'have cut man in two, setting one half against the other', Galt tells the nation.

> They have taught him that his body and his consciousness are two enemies engaged in deadly conflict, two antagonists of opposite natures, contradictory claims, incompatible needs, that to benefit one is to injure the other, that his soul belongs to a supernatural realm, but his body is an evil prison holding it in bondage on this earth […] (*AS*: 1026)

Neither Rand nor her heroes agree with the dualists' proposition. There is no 'supernatural dimension', she herself insists in an introduction to *The Fountainhead*, thus ruling out the possibility that a transcendent world exists which mortals might hope to enter after death. Just as she attacked religion's monopolization of the field of ethics, in which clerics placed the highest moral concepts of our language 'outside this earth and beyond man's reach' (*F*: xi), so too in the field of metaphysics she undermined religion by asserting, through Galt, that man is 'an indivisible entity of matter and consciousness' (*AS*: 1029). Her monism underpins atheism by precluding the presence of a divine being in her philosophy and focusing attention exclusively on humankind in the observable material world humans inhabit. It bears repeating that Rand's view of religion as the 'great poison of mankind',[14] which echoes the Marxian characterization of religion as the 'opium of the people', is at odds with the traditional conservative identification of America as a Christian nation which patriots ask God to bless.

Secondly, though, Rand rejects determinism of various kinds which had been introduced into Russia in the mid-nineteenth century through the writings of certain Western European philosophers, social thinkers and physiologists. In this respect, she opposes the intellectual orthodoxy of the radical intelligentsia of the age of Alexander II, when it became fashionable to believe with the Left-wing Hegelian philosopher Ludwig Feuerbach, for example, that 'man is what he eats'.[15] Rand undermines such ideas by having them parroted by characters

71

of whom she clearly disapproves. As a prominent businessman, who does not speak for her, observes in *The Fountainhead*, humans are 'all just a lot of glands and chemicals and whatever we ate for breakfast' (*F*: 657–8). In *Atlas Shrugged*, this physiological determinism is preached by Dr Pritchett, the head of the department of philosophy at a major university and one of Rand's detested intellectuals. Pritchett regards 'man' as 'just a collection of chemicals with delusions of grandeur' and preposterous 'metaphysical pretensions', a 'miserable bit of protoplasm' (*AS*: 131). Other characters in Rand's novels take up equally deterministic ideas about the role of environment in shaping human behaviour, ideas to which the Russian radical intelligentsia and Marxists more generally had also been partial. Chernyshevsky had crudely argued, for example, that it was 'circumstances' in people's lives that accounted for their choice of work and the extent to which they were 'good' or 'bad'.[16] Similarly, the former head of a failed corporation tries to persuade Dagny, in *Atlas Shrugged*, 'that man is made by the material factors of his background, and that a man's mind is shaped by his tools of production' (*AS*: 320). In *The Fountainhead*, Toohey invokes both physiological and environmental determinism when he opines that 'we are merely the creatures of our chemical metabolism and of the economic factors of our background' (*F*: 594). For Rand, such deterministic ideas have extremely detrimental effects. If, as Dr Ferris believes, a 'man's brain is a social product', just a 'sum of influences that he's picked up from those around him' (*AS*: 540), then responsibility for life's outcomes would rest chiefly with the state rather than the individual. The worth of the human personality would be correspondingly small, and socialists would be vindicated.

To accept the pessimistic determinism that characterizes so many of Rand's inferior beings would be to overlook the faculties of reason and volition, which all humans possess but which only people of her higher category can be relied upon to exercise. It follows that when she turns to a third philosophical question that animated the Russian intelligentsia, the role of reason in human affairs, Rand takes the view to which radical thinkers inclined that humans were rational beings capable of thought unclouded by faith or feeling or any other source of irrational assumptions. Deluded intellectuals in her novels, such as

Dr Pritchett and Dr Ferris, dismiss the faculty of reason as 'the most naïve of all superstitions' or even as 'an irrational idea' (*AS*: 132, 340), but for the Randian hero reason is humans' unique possession and 'means of survival' (*AS*: 1012). Everything humans are and everything they have, Roark asserts in *The Fountainhead*, comes from 'a single attribute of man – the function of his reasoning mind' (*F*: 711). Galt develops the point in *Atlas Shrugged*, the principal theme of which, Rand subsequently stated, was the 'role of the mind in man's existence'.[17] The mind, Galt proclaims, is the essential attribute of the self, or rather 'the independent mind that recognizes no authority higher than its own and no value higher than its judgment of truth' (*AS*: 1030). 'I am', Galt declares, twisting Descartes, 'therefore I'll think' (*AS*: 1058).[18]

As he comes to this conclusion, Galt would seem to be engaging with a Russian literary antagonist, Dostoevsky's 'underground man', who – in *Notes from Underground* (1864) – insisted that he wished to satisfy his whole nature, not just his 'reasoning capacity', which constituted only 'some twentieth part of [his] total capacity for life'. In order to express the irrational side of his nature, Dostoevsky's rebel inveighs against the finality of the equation $2 \times 2 = 4$ and challenges the iron laws of mathematics, which were so highly respected in the age of scientific and industrial progress. Perhaps $2 \times 2 = 5$ might be no bad thing, he speculates.[19] Galt takes up the challenge as he outlines the choice he believes people must make between fulfilling their highest potential, on the one hand, and the unreason that dooms them to a sub-human existence, on the other. For Galt, of course, the correct choice is to accept 'the fact that the noblest act you have ever performed is the act of your mind in the process of grasping that two and two make four' (*AS*: 1058). Rand's perfect being (like Chernyshevsky's) intends to apply his reason to all the problems he faces, including his relations with fellow humans.

While they possess reason, humans still have to choose whether to use this faculty, and here we come to a further metaphysical preoccupation of Rand's. The question of free will or volition (*volia*) had exercised Chernyshevsky, who played down its role in human behaviour in his polemical articles[20] but found himself in need of it when he came to portray Rakhmetov, a proto-revolutionary who was planning to change the course of history. Many villains or inferior beings among Rand's characters believe humans have weak volition. Toohey, for example, had gone so far as to contend in a book on architecture that 'there was no such thing as free will, since men's creative urges were determined, as all else, by the economic structure of the epoch in which they lived' (*F*: 70). Such a view engenders pessimism, resignation, fatalism and an inevitabilist view of history. Rand's heroes, like the typical Russian positive hero or Bolshevik activist in Socialist Realist fiction, take the opposite view. As Galt puts it, '*man is a being of volitional consciousness*', so that for an authentic human being the question 'to be or not to be' is the question 'to think or not to think' (*AS*: 1012; Rand's italics). Such beings must use their will as well as their reasoning minds to realize their egos as fully as they can. In the absence of eternal life in a transcendent world, that can be their only goal in this earthly vale.

CHAPTER 5

POLITICS AND ECONOMICS

An anarchist's utopia?

Rand's corrupted scientist Robert Stadler, who had once believed in the unlimited power of reason, comes to the view, in *Atlas Shrugged*, that humans 'cannot be reached by a rational argument'. Faced with the obtuseness of the common herd, he arrives at a similar conclusion to that reached by Shigalev in Dostoevsky's *Devils* and the Grand Inquisitor whom Ivan Karamazov imagines in Dostoevsky's last novel. In return for material security, the masses must accept totalitarian government. 'If we want to accomplish anything', Stadler argues, 'we have to deceive [the governed] into letting us accomplish it. Or force them' (*AS*: 191).

In contrast with the totalitarian state envisaged by some Dostoevskian characters and accepted with resignation by Stadler, Rand's ideal community seems at first sight to be a libertarian paradise. We might even believe that the inhabitants of Galt's Gulch practise a kind of anarchism. That is to say, no coercive government is necessary there because humans are by nature cooperative beings who are well disposed towards their neighbours and have sufficient resources for everyone who cares to work hard enough to exploit them. Despite the individualistic instinct Rand wishes to unleash, it turns out that 'man *is* a social being' (*AS*: 747; Rand's italics). Individuals – or rather, certain individuals, extraordinary beings – are therefore able to live in the sort of community of which Tolstoy dreamed, without institutions such as armies, police forces, bureaucracies, codes of laws, established churches or the agents of official religions, or at least with only minimalist versions of some of these institutions. As Galt explains to Dagny when she crash-lands her small plane in Galt's Gulch, having followed a plane Galt has piloted there, 'we have no laws in this valley, no rules, no formal organization of any kind' (*AS*: 714). This happy condition is possible because all the inhabitants of Atlantis, as Rand and her characters also call this community, recognize the doctrine of rational self-interest. As the banker Mulligan explains:

> We are not a state here, not a society of any kind – we're just a voluntary association of men held together by nothing but every man's self-interest. I own the valley and I sell the land to the others, when they want it. Judge Narragansett [another refugee from the dystopian world outside Atlantis; DO] is to act as our arbiter, in case of disagreements. He hasn't had to be called upon, as yet. They say that it's hard for men to agree. You'd be surprised how easy it is – when both parties hold as their moral absolute that neither exists for the sake of the other and that reason is their only means of trade. (*AS*: 747–8)

As far as governance is concerned, Rand's utopia is curiously similar to the community in which Engels imagined people would live after a period of dictatorship of the proletariat: the state would have died out because there would no longer be an underclass that the ruling class needed to exploit and repress. The fundamental difference between the Marxian and Randian utopias, of course, is that in the former the means of production would be collectively owned, whereas in the latter they would be privately owned by members of the plutocracy who had considered themselves victimized under the old regime.[1]

Rand's description of her utopian community functions as a political coda to her mid-twentieth-century contribution to the debate about ethics that had unfolded in the pre-revolutionary Russian intelligentsia. Chernyshevsky had argued that humans, being rational creatures, could be persuaded that it was to their advantage to take account of the interests of others, especially the interests of underprivileged majorities, and that they would benefit from the ensuing social harmony in cooperative socialist communities. Dostoevsky believed that humans had a natural propensity to love others and might bring about a spiritual utopia if, like his monastic elder Father Zosima in *The Brothers Karamazov*, they humbly acknowledged their sinfulness and renounced the selfish ambitions that drove them to ill-treat others. People would not reach that happy state and cease to do evil things, though, merely as a result of exposure to enlightened people who could explain to them what was in their best interests. It was naïve to assume, Dostoevsky's 'underground man' complained with Chernyshevsky in mind, that humans always wish to do what is good for them, for in fact they often behave perversely, in ways that are harmful to others or to themselves, in order to demonstrate their freedom of action.[2] Rand, for her part, denied that it was either rational or natural for humans to love their neighbours as themselves. Consequently, her capitalist utopia is founded on the assumption that the best means of removing all the causes of conflict that have bedevilled human societies through the ages is to allow rational men (the inhabitants of her utopia are almost all men, and all of them suppose that they are rational) to pursue without restraint the goals they set themselves.

Rand's fictional account of a utopia underpinned by her version of rational egoism has several striking weaknesses. In the first place, many readers will surely find Rand's literary characterization psychologically implausible. She expects us to believe that among rational men there will all of a sudden be 'no victims and no conflicts of interest', because such men, Galt explains, 'do not desire the unearned and do not view one another with a cannibal's lust' (*AS*: 1022). We are invited to assume that the enterprising, self-driven, competitive, ruthless and sometimes violent men who make bargains only on their own terms, once they are gathered together in Atlantis, will amicably cooperate with one another. Perhaps this assumption seems reasonable to Rand because it rests on the premise that all human relationships resemble nothing so much as commercial transactions. Galt believes that the 'symbol of all relationships among [rational] men, the moral symbol of respect for human beings, is *the trader*' (*AS*: 1022; Rand's italics). Utopia as Rand conceives of it must therefore offer a 'free, productive, rational system which demands and rewards the best in every man', in other words laissez-faire capitalism, an unregulated free market (*F*: ix). This moral to her story is pointed up as the novel glides towards its happy ending. As Rand's heroes relax serenely in Atlantis after the old world has fallen, Narragansett formulates a single new clause to be added to the American Constitution: 'Congress shall make no law abridging the freedom of production and trade' (*AS*: 1168).

In the second place, one may point to instances in which Rand's heroes themselves breach the few restrictions on their freedom of action that they theoretically accept. The 'only proper purpose of a government', Galt argues in his broadcast to the nation,

> is to protect man's rights, which means: to protect him from physical violence. A proper government is only a policeman, acting as an agent of man's self-defense, and, as such, may resort to force *only* against those who *start* the use of force. (*AS*: 1062; Rand's italics)

The declaration of this pacific non-initiation or non-aggression principle seems to justify the self-righteousness that Rand's heroes and she herself display, warranting their presentation of themselves as victims who respond forcefully only to physical threats. It is a piece of evidence to which Barbara Branden points in defence of Rand's outlook. Unlike Nietzsche, Branden contends, Rand 'rejected as unforgivably immoral any suggestion that the superior man had the right to employ physical force as a means to his end'.[3] Branden makes this claim in an attempt to convince readers that Rand did not intend words that she put in the mouth of Kira in the original version of *We the Living* to be taken literally. Although she loathed the Bolsheviks' ideals, Kira tells her communist lover Andrei, she admired their method. 'If one believes one's right, one shouldn't wait to convince millions of fools, one might just as well force them', she supposes, although she is not sure whether she would 'include blood' in her methods.[4]

And yet, there is abundant evidence in both Rand's major novels that runs counter to the claim that Rand is consistently committed to the non-initiation principle. Randian heroes do habitually resort to first use of force, destroying property and attacking or threatening to attack other individuals if violence promotes their goals, or if they are thwarted by non-violent means, or feel aggrieved, or simply wish to have their own way. Roark, in *The Fountainhead*, destroys a building with explosives because he finds, when he returns to New York after a long absence, that the condition on which he had allowed it to be built – namely, that the building should conform in every detail to his design – had been disregarded (*F*: Part 4, chapter 12). He is also a rapist. His act of sexual violence against Dominique Francon, who is to become his seemingly predestined partner, is a premeditated assertion of his right to self-fulfilment and his desire to master Dominique (*F*: 221, 257, 263, 703).[5] Rand's approval of first use of force continues to find expression in *Atlas Shrugged*. Dagny, for example, threatens to 'complete the family legend', which goes back to her grandfather Nathaniel, by killing any politician who tried to refuse a permission that one should never have had to ask (*AS*: 197).

Rand found ingenious reasons to excuse law-breaking by her superheroes. She believed, for instance, that aggrieved industrialists and businessmen were entitled to resist payment of taxes because the state could collect taxes at the point of a gun and taxation itself therefore amounted to an initiation of physical force.[6] The behaviour that Rand licenses when dealing with her heroes thus seems essentially indistinguishable from that which she condemns in the strongest terms when dealing with her ideological enemies, such as a journalist on her doomed train who believes that 'it is proper and moral to use compulsion "for a good cause"' (*AS*: 605). It turns out that the morality Rand considers absolute and objective rests on trust in her own evaluation of the character and ideology of the person whose action she is judging – a position reminiscent of the moral relativism on which Dostoevsky's Raskol'nikov based the right of his 'extraordinary' men to kill.

The exclusivity of Rand's New Jerusalem

A third and even more serious weakness of the utopian community that Rand presents to readers in *Atlas Shrugged* (from the point of view of a majority of humans, at least) is its exclusivity. Atlantis is a refuge for a chosen few, not for the common run of humankind. The virtuous men who have set it up, its founding fathers as it were, have undertaken a process of selection in order to ensure that all its members subscribe to the rational ethical values those founders have laid down. No 'sub-animal creatures who crawl on their bellies, grunting that there is no mind' (*AS*: 715), are to be found here, Dagny is told by a young physicist who has chosen to follow Galt. Altruism, the willing subordination of self to others, has no place either. Consequently, there is a word 'which is forbidden in this valley', Galt forewarns Dagny: 'the word "*give*"' (*AS*: 714; Rand's italics). Dagny accordingly receives a wage, whether she likes it or not, for cooking Galt's breakfast, a simple everyday task in which she unexpectedly takes pleasure in this bracing moral atmosphere (*AS*: 753, 759–61).

Rand's utopian community, then, is highly inaccessible, and not just because it is sealed off by its natural geographical barriers and artful camouflage. As a participant in a social conversation early in the novel has heard, the Atlantis of legend, after which Rand's utopia is named, is 'a place where hero-spirits lived in a happiness unknown to the rest of the earth. A place which only the spirits of heroes could enter, and they reached it without dying, because they carried the secret of life within them' (*AS*: 153). Galt, a bearer of this secret, confirms at the end of his broadcast that when he and his band of destroyers reclaim their great country from 'the impotent savages who never discovered its nature, its meaning, its splendor', they will open the gates of their city to 'those who deserve to enter' (*AS*: 1067) – but not, it follows, to everybody who hopes for a place in the sun. Presumably, none of the second-raters, second-handers, bums, goons, rotters or ideological opponents whom Rand's heroes despise will ever gain admission. Like the New Jerusalem prophesied in the Book of Revelation, this community is for 'them which are saved', but 'there shall in no wise enter into it any thing that defileth, neither *whatsoever* worketh abomination, or *maketh* a lie'.[7]

Nor, it seems, will many of that half of the human race who happen to be female – to whose rights the Russian radical intelligentsia paid so much attention and whose capabilities it acknowledged – be able to enter Rand's paradise. From what we see of Atlantis, women are barely represented there. Dagny, as Rand's alter ego in the novel, is welcome, of course. Ragnar's wife, Kay Ludlow, a renowned and glamorous actress, is a member too, and her performance in a play Dagny attends edifies the community's spectators. However, Rand seems unwittingly to underline Kay's (and women's) relative unimportance when she grants readers a glimpse of her Titans at rest after their triumphant exploits at the end of the novel. As Ragnar (who, despite his prowess as a pirate, yearns to be a philosopher!) peruses a volume of Aristotle, Kay engages in what Rand evidently sees as a more fitting female activity: she 'sat before a mirror, thoughtfully studying the shades of film make-up' (*AS*: 1167). Nor is it expected that many other women will qualify for membership of this community. As Ragnar candidly tells Dagny when she unexpectedly turns up there, she is the only woman left in the outer world who would be allowed to enter it (*AS*: 754).

The noticeable dearth of women in Atlantis is probably due to 'feminine helplessness'[8] or other deficiencies which Rand seems to attribute to the female psyche. It is not just liberals and socialists who have no respect for women, that is to say men like the novelist Balph Eubank, who sees Dagny as 'a symptom of the illness of our century', 'a woman who runs a railroad, instead of practicing the beautiful craft of the handloom and bearing children' (*AS*: 138). The omniscient Francisco shows similar condescension. 'I wish I could tell you what a relief it is', he confides to Dagny, 'to see a face that's intelligent though a woman's' (*AS*: 118). Rand herself observes, when she describes the unusual spectacle of Dagny in an evening gown, that a diamond band on the wrist of Dagny's naked arm 'gave her the most feminine of all aspects: the look of being chained' (*AS*: 136). It is the fate, indeed the desire, of Rand's heroines – and of Rand herself[9] – to be sexually dominated by the men whose drive and genius they admire. Acceptance of a subordinate role was consistent with Rand's belief, as Barbara Branden reports it, that the essence of femininity was hero-worship, the desire to look up to a man.[10] Women even seem ideologically suspect, for Rand codes leftism, it has been suggested, as 'effeminate, and unnatural'.[11]

Viewed in this light, attempts to treat Rand as a feminist writer whose heroines provide models for women in need of emancipation seem ill-conceived.[12] She herself, according to Branden, was an 'anti-feminist' who 'regarded man as a superior value' and was delighted to learn that someone had called her 'the most courageous *man* in America'. She also opposed the feminist movement because many of its representatives, she believed, exhibited the collectivist orientation she detested.[13] If *What Is to Be Done?* served as an early feminist text, then, Rand's definitive work envisions a new form of male hegemony. In this respect, as in others, Rand turns upside down the utopian dream of Russian radicals in which men and women were equal partners – a dream symbolized in communist times by a monument created for the Soviet pavilion at the World's Fair of 1937 in Paris in which a (male) proletarian bearing a hammer was linked to a (female) peasant wielding a sickle.

Atlantis thus resembles a celibate monastic community. It is an austere and mirthless place where embittered men, clad in the armour of rational egoism, all agree with one another and lead purely transactional existences. Unlike the utopias imagined by Russian thinkers, whether they were positioned at the radical socialist or the conservative nationalist end of the political spectrum, it is also devoid of any organic social unit that might bind together and give shelter to groups within the larger community. It is striking, for example, that although *Atlas Shrugged* is a novel of epic proportions with a cast of characters comparable in extent to that of *War and Peace*, no multi-generational Tolstoyan family, happy or unhappy, is to be found in it. In fact, children are almost absent from this otherwise panoramic reflection on human life, except insofar as the principals themselves were once children. (Galt, incidentally, is an orphan, and it is perhaps equally significant that Roark, in *The Fountainhead*, is not aware that he has any close relatives (*F*: 14).) In Atlantis itself, Dagny sees only two children, boys aged seven and four, who are the sons of the woman who runs the bakery. The virtual absence of children here is explained to Dagny by the boys' mother: 'there can be no collective commitments in this valley and […] families or relatives are not allowed to come here, unless each person takes the striker's oath by his own independent conviction.' The baker herself, who is married to one of the male residents in Atlantis, has been admitted to the community in her own right to practise the profession of motherhood, so that she may bring up her sons 'as human beings', which it is apparently impossible to do 'in the outer world', where educational systems are 'devised to stunt a child's brain' and 'convince him that reason is impotent' (*AS*: 784–5).

It is easy to see why a writer of Rand's limited insight into human character might avoid the literary challenge of exploring the psychology of a child, which Tolstoy investigated so profoundly. As an aspiring political visionary, on the other hand, Rand was perhaps unwise to ignore the question of how her race of supermen would propagate itself and educate its offspring. The immediate purpose of her utopia, to be sure, is to accommodate in a supposedly rational and peaceable community the aggressive males of whom she dreams. Working in their self-interested way with the abundant natural resources of the terrain they would control after the revolution they had organized, these men – Rand might persuade some readers – would bring humans to an unprecedented level of technological mastery of their environment. It is harder, though, to convince readers that the emotionally barren community these men had taken such pains to bring into being, at such cost in human suffering, economic damage and political turmoil, would survive beyond the revolutionary generation without paying some attention to procreation and pedagogy. Or at least, many readers are bound to wonder whether such a community could survive without the construction of a state just as repressive as the homeland from which Rand had fled and which always served in her landscape as the polar opposite of her utopia.

Democracy and economic distribution in Rand's ideal world

We cannot be sure, from Rand's fictional outline of her ideal community, whether post-revolutionary Atlantis is to remain an enclave as cut off from the outside world as Zamiatin's unitary state in his novel *We* is by the Green Wall that surrounds it. If any ordinary humans remain alive after the apocalypse Galt and his fellow revolutionaries have set in train, perhaps Atlantis will become an imperial headquarters from which colonies of inferior beings will be ruled. Or perhaps Rand's savages in the world outside Atlantis will die out, for they do not have the capacity to use reason and exercise the volition that potentially distinguishes humans from all other living species. Two things *are* clear, though, about the nature of any future community, self-contained or imperial, of which Rand would approve.

The first certainty is that democracy will not function in a Randian utopia in the way to which Western readers were accustomed in Rand's time and which many of them still wish to preserve in the twenty-first century. Among the passengers on Rand's ill-fated train of whom she is highly critical is an elderly school-teacher who had 'spent her life turning class after class of helpless children into miserable cowards, by teaching them that the will of the majority is the only standard of good and evil, that a majority may do anything it pleases' (*AS*: 605). This disrespect for the will of the majority implies a negative attitude towards Western European representative institutions which was commonplace at both the conservative and radical ends of the political spectrum in the pre-revolutionary Russian intelligentsia. Herzen, Chernyshevsky and Dostoevsky, for example, were all critical of contemporary parliamentary institutions in France and Britain. At the radical end of the spectrum in particular, the term 'democracy' had a positive connotation when it was construed as government *in the supposed interests* of the common people, but not when it was understood as election of representatives of the people through extensive or universal adult suffrage. To any observer who believes that a government derives its legitimacy from its ability to secure a majority of votes from an electorate, Rand's indifference to majority opinion may seem anti-democratic, even un-American, but it sits comfortably in the Russian political tradition.

Rand's aversion to representative democracy, irrespective of whether it is coloured by attitudes in the Russian intelligentsia, is a corollary of her division of humans into the ordinary and the extraordinary. She was already pondering the political implications of her taxonomy of humankind in notes she made in 1934 on a new conception of the state that she wanted to defend. The state for her should be a means to an end, 'a means for the convenience of the higher type of man'.

The fault of 'liberal democracies', she observed, was 'giving full rights to quantity (majorities)' and forgetting 'the rights of quality, which are much higher rights'.[14] In later notes that she wrote, in 1947, for the 'philosophical conclusion' of *Atlas Shrugged*, on which she had by then embarked, she effectively ruled out the possibility that her extraordinary men would be prepared to hand power back to the benighted mass of deluded second-raters they had just defeated. 'From now on', she reminded herself, 'the exploitation of the best by the worst will never again be permitted by the best'.[15] It is therefore quite unclear who would be eligible to sit in the Congress whose powers would be limited by the amendment to the US Constitution that Narragansett formulates at the very end of the novel or how congressmen would be elected in Rand's post-revolutionary world. Surely Rand's extraordinary humans, having devoted their formidable reasoning capacity, will-power and organizational skills to the overthrow of the greedy, self-serving liberal establishment, would not allow all adult Americans to stand or vote in new presidential and congressional elections. As for the habit of compromise, the negotiated give and take on which democratic politics depends if it is to function smoothly, Randian heroes such as Roark and Galt consider it a contemptible betrayal of the self-respecting ego.

The second certainty about a Randian utopia is that in a society where the notion of a general, public interest has been rejected and where humans are free to pursue their economic interests as they see fit, the question of economic distribution, which democratic institutions spend much time debating, will already have been definitively settled. Social justice, for Rand, consists in the entitlement of those individuals who drive the economy to retain all the profits derived from their enterprise. Although Rand's industrious heroes are motivated not so much by materialism (in the sense of enjoyment of financial success) as by their perfectionism and thirst for self-realization, they do expect to receive all the earnings generated by their inventiveness and energy. Roark resents the levying of taxes to fund social welfare. Rearden is possessive about his profit (*AS*: 480–1). Galt, when asked by the nation's president for advice on how to resolve the economic crisis to which his strike has reduced the

United States, suggests in a similar vein that the government 'start by abolishing all income taxes' (*AS*: 1101). Nor will Rand's heroes tolerate government regulation, labour unions or – as Francisco expresses Rand's sentiments – 'tax-collecting vermin' (*AS*: 766). Ragnar, for his part, is outraged by the romantic idealization of Robin Hood, whom Rand, it has been suggested, may have regarded as a model for the Bolsheviks who expropriated the property of her own relatively well-to-do family.[16] In Ragnar's estimation, the medieval English outlaw is not 'a moral ideal' but 'the foulest of creatures', a leech who lived 'on the blood of the rich' (*AS*: 576–7). If Rand is to recommend any economic redistribution, then, it will favour the humans of her higher category of beings, not the undeserving mass in her lower category. Humble manual labourers are reminded how much they already owe to the men of excellence who have created the jobs that provide their livelihoods and how small is the reward they deserve for their physical contributions to production in industrial society (*AS*: 1064).

Thus, in *Atlas Shrugged*, Rand moves beyond the urge of the exceptional man to realize himself to the full, which she had already illustrated in *The Fountainhead*, and explores the political and economic dimensions of her full-blown rational egoism. A world fit for her heroes will liberate them from whatever political and economic curbs have been placed on them. Rand's unabashed division of humankind into higher and lower categories precludes a commitment to maintain democracy as a majoritarian electoral system. Perhaps she would have endorsed the view expressed by an American Republican senator in 2020 that 'democracy isn't the objective; liberty, peace and prosperity are. We want the human condition to flourish. Rank democracy can thwart that'.[17] As for the version of capitalist enterprise under which Rand would want heroes to live, it would resemble the version recently described by George Monbiot as 'warlord capitalism'. Liberty, in this scenario, 'turns out to mean total freedom for plutocrats': 'all restraints on accumulation', such as 'taxes, regulations and the public ownership of essential services', would be regarded as illegitimate, and nothing 'should be allowed to stand in the way of profit-making'.[18]

CHAPTER 6

GEOPOLITICS

Russia and Europe in Russian thought

It remains to consider Rand's responses to certain overarching questions that had preoccupied the Russian intelligentsia since long before her novels were written, questions about the destinies of civilizations and their inter-relationships. Acutely conscious of Russia's marginal position in the European world, pre-revolutionary Russian thinkers and writers anxiously compared cultures and constructed paradigms for discussion of them. Since the age of Peter the Great, who had tried to modernize the backward state he inherited by Europeanizing its armed forces, administration, nobility and cultural practices so that it could compete effectively in the European arena, 'Europe' or 'the West' had been a major landmark in the universe of the small educated minority. Behind almost every facet of speculation about the 'accursed questions' in late imperial Russia, there lay a concern about Russia's relation to the Western European civilization from which it had borrowed heavily and about the nature of Russia's own identity. Was Russia's culture poor and imitative or rich and original? Was Russia destined to follow more advanced civilizations or to transcend them and lead a new civilization of its own making? Classical Russian thought was accordingly distinguished by a rich tradition of quasi-philosophical speculation about the course of history and what we should now call geopolitics. Thinkers and writers looked for evidence of providential design and human agency, pattern in historical development, teleological explanations of national destiny and clashes of civilizations.

Nineteenth-century conservative nationalists, keen to assert Russia's cultural exceptionalism and to assign their country a unique historical mission, drew a sharp distinction between the supposedly peace-loving Russian people, whose Orthodox piety reflected their brotherly Christian natures and social instincts, and the allegedly aggressive, materialistic and individualistic peoples of the West. Exponents of this contrastive paradigm appeared in several phases. The so-called Slavophiles (most notably Konstantin Aksakov, Aleksei Khomiakov and Ivan Kireevsky) and Official Nationalists (especially Mikhail Pogodin) flourished from the late 1830s to the mid-1850s. Native-Soil Conservatives (Dostoevsky and others) followed in their footsteps in the early 1860s. In the later 1860s, Nikolai Danilevsky applied the principle of binary opposition to the analysis of cultures or civilizations in his magnum opus *Russia and Europe* (1869). In the 1870s, Pan-Slavists used this sort of nationalism with militaristic intent for imperial expansion in Central Asia and the Balkans.

By contrast, the more amorphous and politically diverse group of so-called Westernizers, which at one time or another included Belinsky, Herzen, Turgenev, Chernyshevsky and others, sought to represent Russia as a European nation. Russia, the Westernizers argued, needed to draw on what they variously regarded as the best features of the cultures of their more highly developed Western neighbours in order to overcome the country's chronic historical backwardness. For some Westernizers (for instance, Belinsky in his last years, Chernyshevsky and Pisarev), Western European achievements included the articulation of the socialist ideas which Charles Fourier, Robert Owen, Étienne Cabet, Louis Blanc and many others had begun to propagate in the first half of the nineteenth century. Herzen in particular found early European non-Marxian socialism attractive and exploited the Russia-versus-the-West paradigm as a means of presenting his own nation as the place where a collectivist utopia might first come into being. Russia, in Herzen's imagination, was a 'new world' which could surpass the dying 'old' world of 'Europe' by serving as a laboratory for the implementation of socialist ideas that had supposedly been ingrained in the Russian peasantry for centuries. Herzen outlined his view of Russia as a revivifying force in his cycles of essays *Letters from France and Italy* and *From the Other Shore*, both of which were published for the first time in complete Russian editions in 1855. In other essays of the same period, he established a nativist tradition of 'Russian Socialism', which was taken up from the late 1860s by 'Populist' revolutionaries.

The conception of Russia as a fresh force enabled classical Russian thinkers (including thinkers at the conservative nationalist end of the spectrum) to reject the pessimistic view of their country that Petr Chaadaev had put forward in a shocking 'Philosophical Letter' published in 1836, at the end of which he characterized Moscow as a necropolis.[1] On the contrary, those who took a more optimistic view of Russia's destiny began to say, it was the West, with its inhuman capitalist economy and acquisitive bourgeoisie, that was moribund. Herzen himself described Rome as 'the greatest cemetery in the world' and reused the image of the West as a graveyard when he analysed the wreckage of the failed European revolutions of 1848.[2] Dostoevsky deployed the same image when, in his last novel, he had Ivan Karamazov tell his brother Alesha that he wished to visit the West, the fountainhead of modern Russian culture, although he knew that he was only going to a graveyard.[3]

Russians' emerging view of their nation as a new world roughly coincided with the growth of their interest in the youthful country at the opposite, occidental extremity of Western civilization, to which the French political writer Alexis de Tocqueville had drawn attention in his highly influential work, *Democracy in America* (1835–40).[4] Herzen himself identified America as one of the two possible heirs, alongside the Slav world, to Europe's rich past.[5] This interest is echoed in *What Is to Be Done?*, inasmuch as Chernyshevsky's Lopukhov, it will be recalled, worked in America after faking his suicide in Russia, and in Dostoevsky's *The Devils*, in which Shatov and Kirillov visit the United States to experience the life of the American worker. Persuaded (only temporarily, in Shatov's case) that Russians were inferior to Americans, these Dostoevskian characters uncritically approved of whatever they found there, including spiritualism, lynchings, private use of firearms and vagrancy.[6] Then, from the late nineteenth century, prominent Russian writers (Vladimir Korolenko in 1893, Gorky in 1906, Mayakovsky in 1925) added the United States to the itinerary of the Russian traveller and left literary accounts of their impressions.[7] America thus entered the set of civilizations (Russia, Europe, the West,

Asia, the old world, the new world) from which Russians constructed frameworks that would enable them, they hoped, to understand their identity and destiny.

A war of the worlds

Of the above-mentioned Russian accounts of visits to the United States, Mayakovsky's *My Discovery of America*, published in full in Russia in August 1926, is of particular interest here, not least because Mayakovsky's visit preceded Rand's arrival in the country by just a few months.[8] His impressions of America may have become known to Rand before she left Leningrad (as Petrograd was renamed after the death of Lenin in 1924) in late January 1926, since some parts of his travelogue were published soon after his return to Moscow in November 1925.[9]

As an exponent of Futurism (an artistic movement whose members were inspired by technological advance and the dynamism of life in the modern city), Mayakovsky was alive to the possibility that the United States might serve as a useful example for the Bolsheviks as they set about modernizing Russia through rapid industrialization and electrification. At the same time, he was disturbed, as a communist, by the economic, social and racial inequality he observed in America. His views on American capitalism follow on smoothly from those of pre-revolutionary Russian radical thinkers about the British and French economic systems. He censures the capitalist, who, 'having separated out and allocated a percentage of workers of material value to himself (certain specialists, tame union bosses, etc.) treats the remaining working masses like inexhaustible goods'.[10] His comments on what he takes to be Americans' attitude towards money, their tendency to rate people by their financial worth and their admiration for their dollar are antithetical to the outline of a philosophy of money that Rand would eventually present in *Atlas Shrugged*.[11]

At the end of his account of his trip to the United States, Mayakovsky contemplates the possibility of a clash between American civilization and Russian civilization. 'It could happen', he supposes, that the United States will 'turn out to be the final armed defenders of a hopeless bourgeois cause – then history will be able to write a good Wellsian novel of *The War of the Worlds*'. Despite his ideological commitment to Bolshevism, he takes quite a balanced view of the contrast between the old and the new worlds which will shortly vie with one another. The qualitative difference between the dynamic new American world and the declining old European world is captured in a scene Mayakovsky witnesses when the French ship that brings him back to Europe at the end of his trip docks at Le Havre and in his subsequent onward journey to Paris. In Le Havre, ragged cripples and urchins gather on the quay to fight over the small change that passengers throw from the ship's decks, a scene which amuses the Americans on board and which they record in snapshots. These French beggars are imprinted in Mayakovsky's imagination 'as a symbol of the Europe to come – if there is no cessation of the grovelling before American – and anyone else's – money'. His journey by road through Normandy then gives rise to conflicting thoughts. 'By comparison with America, you see pitiful shacks here', he admits. 'Every inch of land has been seized through age-old struggle, has been exhausted through the ages', and has been used to grow violets or lettuce. And yet, even this 'contemptible attachment to the cottage, to the strip of land, to what is one's own', strikes him as 'a prodigious culture' in comparison to the temporary, improvised nature and 'self-seeking character' of American life. On the other hand, how quickly the West could fall behind America technologically: 'all the way to Rouen, along the endless chestnut-lined country roads, going through the densest patch in France, we met only one automobile'.[12]

Rand shares Mayakovsky's vision of modernity as urban and highly industrialized, and she too anticipates a war of the worlds. However, her evaluation of the two sides in this impending conflict is diametrically opposed to Mayakovsky's and even more sharply polarized. The economic systems of the two worlds, their methods of production and distribution, their notions of justice, the moral values that will underpin their societies and polities, the psychological needs of the humans who will inhabit them – all are irreconcilably different in Rand's account. Nor will Rand's revolutionary vanguard ever contemplate peaceful co-existence.

Ayn Rand and the Russian Intelligentsia

Making America great again

How, finally, does Rand reorganize the Russia-versus-Europe paradigm offered in the corpus of Russian thought that helped to shape her mind in her youth in order to produce a geopolitical view which served the interests of her adoptive land and spiritual home?

In her first novel, Rand refers explicitly to the controversy between Slavophiles and Westernizers and stands with the latter group, having her egoist Leo Kovalensky acknowledge 'the superiority of Western culture over that of Russia' and making him goad ageing diplomats who were 'rabid Slavophiles' (*WL*: 122). Her view of Russia during the part of her life she spent there, as she explained it to Barbara Branden, was of a 'stupid, backward, mystical, and sentimental' country. 'It was the West – especially England in her early years, when she knew little of America – that was her ideal', because that was where 'civilization', that is to say 'intellectual, rational people', was to be found.[13]

By the time she wrote her major novels, Rand had evidently come to regard Russia not as a civilizational type that was distinct from 'Europe' but as a barely habitable satellite of it. In a personal afterword that she wrote to *Atlas Shrugged*, she prefers to associate herself with the continental whole rather than the specific country where she had been brought up, disavowing the entire continent in the process. 'I was born in Europe' (i.e. in St Petersburg), she tells her readers, 'but I came to America because this was the country based on my moral premises and the only country where one could be fully free to write. I came here alone, after graduating from a European college' (i.e. the University of Petrograd). She makes no mention of her Russian background, it will be noted, presenting herself as a refugee from a civilization which, *pace* numerous members of the Russian intelligentsia, she considers essentially European and damaged by moral and political defects that are common to many nations. She also sets up a contrast (yet another binary opposition) between the depraved Europe she has left behind and America, to which she truly belongs, she claims, 'by choice and conviction' (*AS*: [1170]). The opposition between Russia and Europe, which was one of the dominant rhetorical motifs of pre-revolutionary

Russian thought and literature, is thus turned into an opposition between Europe and America.

As an intellectual formed in the crucible of revolutionary Petrograd, where she acquired the habit of thinking about national essence and destiny in simple contrastive terms, Rand incorporated her negative view of Russia into the notion of Europe that readers encounter in her two major novels. Her anti-hero Ellsworth Toohey is already explicitly pointing out the essential, collectivist, totalitarian similarity of Russia to other parts of Europe in *The Fountainhead*. One country, Toohey asserts with the USSR in its Stalinist phase in mind, 'is dedicated to the proposition that man has no rights, that the collective is all. The individual held as evil, the mass – as God. No motive and no virtue permitted – except that of service to the proletariat'. In Hitler's Germany too, humans have no rights and 'the State is all. The individual held as evil, the race – as God. No motive and no virtue permitted – except that of service to the race' (*F*: 669).[14] In Rand's outlook, then, Russia (past and present) is not so much an entity that is *sui generis* as a historically inferior component of a continent that is becoming uniform.

Admittedly, nowhere in the world is unaffected by the horrors Rand thinks she identifies. Oriental civilizations are all repellent to the heroes who represent her views. Some of them, such as the People's State of China and the People's State of Turkey, seem to have become socialist dystopias. Galt sweepingly denounces the 'barefoot bum in some pesthole of Asia' who rants at Americans for daring to be rich and he deplores 'the mystic muck of India' (*AS*: 1055, 1056). All the same, the nidus of the disease that was diverting Rand's new homeland from the path trodden by its freedom-loving founders is Europe, which looms as large in *Atlas Shrugged* as it does in the consciousness of the pre-revolutionary Russian intelligentsia. Europe's unspeakable 'People's States' have become 'wastelands', full of black-market traders, where 'the best men', according to Ragnar, have 'had no choice but to become criminals' (*AS*: 152, 578). These states, Galt complains, are 'slave pens' to whose 'thugs' Americans have been foolishly deferential. 'In the presence of that monument to human morality, which is a factory, a highway or a bridge', Americans have damned their country for its alleged immorality and greed and have kept offering apologies for its 'greatness to the idol of primordial starvation, to decaying Europe's idol of a leprous, mystic bum' (*AS*: 1055, 1056, 1061).

In the last analysis, the choice confronting humankind in the twentieth century, in Rand's opinion, is therefore a choice between Europe and America, which is a beacon for Rand, in much the same way that pre-Petrine Russia had been for pre-revolutionary Russian nationalists and Western Europe had been for Russian Westernizers. America, Roark declares to the jurors who at the end of *The Fountainhead* will acquit him of demolishing the building which had not been erected exactly in accordance with his design, has been the 'noblest country in the history of men. The country of greatest achievement, greatest prosperity, greatest freedom' (*F*: 715). In *Atlas Shrugged*, Rand uses her fictional immigrant, Francisco, to express her opinion about distinctions between cultures and national missions. America's messianic role, according to Francisco, can be best understood by contrast with 'the rest of the earth', of which Europe had been the fulcrum. The dying civilization outside the United States, Francisco explains, has now 'reached the consummation of the beliefs it has held through the ages', namely 'mystic faith' and 'the supremacy of the irrational'. The two monuments that marked the end of its historical journey were the lunatic asylum and the graveyard (*AS*: 771). Rand thus appropriates a favoured Russian image of Europe in its death throes and puts it to fresh use, not to elevate her native land, which is to be consumed in the old world's Armageddon, but to bolster the superior claim of her adoptive land to leadership of the New Jerusalem.

The new American world that Galt's revolution inaugurates in *Atlas Shrugged* comes into being because Rand's heroic minority of men have risen to a higher level of scientific knowledge and technological prowess than humans have previously attained and because they have also developed an unprecedented philosophical understanding of the value they should place on their own egos. However, this utopia is not exclusively forward-thinking, for it also recreates a prelapsarian condition. The post-revolutionary United States will move back to a glorious past by restoring the values of its founding fathers, which had been betrayed by Rand's 'liberal' and 'collectivist' enemies. Like those writers of Imperial Rome who nostalgically imagined the military leaders and legislators of former times as more rugged and less corrupted than their contemporaries, so Rand glorifies the American soldiers and statesmen who fought for the nation's independence and framed its constitution in the late eighteenth century and the frontiersmen who subsequently extended the reach of the early American polity in the nineteenth. The United States, Francisco tells Dagny, 'was the only country in history born, not of chance and blind tribal warfare, but as a rational product of man's mind'. For 'one magnificent century, it redeemed the world. It will have to do so again' (AS: 771). The point is reiterated by Galt in his broadcast to the nation. 'From its start', he explains, 'this country was a threat to the ancient rule of mystics. In the brilliant rocket-explosion of its youth, [it] displayed to an incredulous world what greatness was possible to man, what happiness was possible on earth' (AS: 1061).

Rand's modern American heroes, then, are not only armed with convictions and resolve familiar to readers of the classical Russian novel of ideas and the Socialist Realist novel. They are also endowed with the spirit of the intrepid, buccaneering American pioneer, romanticized by the myth-making studios of Hollywood where Rand worked shortly after her arrival in the United States. In *Atlas Shrugged*, she offers an example of this type in the person of Nathaniel Taggart, Dagny's revered grandfather and the founder of Taggart Transcontinental. Nathaniel 'never accepted the creed that others had the right to stop him', and it was rumoured that in the wilderness of the Mid-West he murdered a state legislator who tried (AS: 59–60). The reincarnation of the frontiersman in the modern world is none other than 'the real maker of wealth, the greatest worker, the highest type of human being – the self-made man – the American industrialist' (AS: 414). Like the Socialist Realist hero, or indeed Stalin ('man of steel') come to that, such men are hard as flint or steel.[15] They are also singularly prone, like Nathaniel, to outbursts of rage if they are obstructed or if their interests or self-respect are threatened. There was 'something about' Ellis Wyatt, for instance, that 'suggested violence' (AS: 81), an impression confirmed by the anger with which he smashes a wine-glass against a wall and sets his oil-wells on fire (*AS*: 250, 335–6). Rand views threats of violence made by her heroes in their private lives with similar equanimity, indeed admiration, as when she reports that Rearden warns his wife, Lillian, that if she ever again mentions his mistress Dagny then he will answer her as he would answer a hoodlum, by beating her up (*AS*: 531). This barely contained aggression is an element of national behaviour that has its origins in another age and at the lawless frontier with the untamed wilderness, but its persistence in modern times seems to Rand to augur well for the country's rebirth.

Thus, revival of America's now threatened values and habits (individualism, drive, pioneering spirit and – when obstacles emerge – readiness to resort to violence) is a paramount task for Rand's intellectual and moral elite in an age of American global ascendancy. In fact, completion of this task, which would bring about the personal transformation of any Americans capable of being saved, is no less important than the patient work Galt and his comrades are doing to undermine the existing dystopian regime. Taken together, accomplishment of these two tasks, one destructive and the other regenerative, would amount to an epoch-making feat, or *podvig*, of the sort for which many a Russian revolutionary or Dostoevskian hero – Alesha Karamazov is an example – yearned.[16]

A successful revolution and the rebirth of civilization in America might also represent the best hope of saving the rest of the world from the mysticism and collectivism to which European civilization has finally succumbed. At the very least, it was in America's own interest to reinstate American values, as the most effective means of protecting this Eden from the corruption that had spread to it from abroad. Galt castigates fellow-Americans in this vein: 'you are letting this greatest of countries be devoured by any scum from any corner of the earth, while you concede that it is selfish to live for your country and that your moral duty is to live for the globe' (*AS*: 1055). It is worth bearing in mind that Rand completed *Atlas Shrugged* during the early years of the Cold War, when Senator Joseph McCarthy was heightening anxiety that communists and Soviet spies had infiltrated American institutions. In October 1947, Rand herself was a willing witness at a sitting of the House Un-American Activities Committee (HUAC), which was investigating suspected communist manipulation of the film industry.[17]

In offering a comprehensive set of answers to aesthetic, ethical, metaphysical, political, social and economic questions of the sort that had fascinated the pre-revolutionary Russian intelligentsia, Rand was thus drawn into consideration of the American national narrative and mission. On this geopolitical level, she presented readers with a contrastive story of the kind that Russian thinkers and writers had told over and over again. Refusing to accept that Russia had made any worthwhile contribution to European civilization, she urged citizens of her adoptive homeland to reject the modern West, which had failed to capitalize on the achievements of the Enlightenment and the nineteenth-century Romantic rebellion, as she idiosyncratically understood them. Instead, her new compatriots – rather like pre-revolutionary Russian nationalists of various hues – should try to recover the golden age through which their country alone had lived. By that means, America might yet avoid the 'cultural sewer' and the 'swamp' of modern philosophy, which was steering nations towards collectivism and totalitarianism,[18] and rediscover the path that led to a unique destiny. By appealing to a better past which had been neglected, disparaged and obscured, Rand stands out as a harbinger of today's populists.[19] Long before them, she was raging against socialism and defending what she called 'Americanism', a doctrine whose 'basic principle' was 'inalienable individual rights' and which could 'be translated into practical reality *only* in the form of the economic system of Free Enterprise'.[20]

CONCLUSION

According to Rand's ethical teaching, altruism is evil, because living for the sake of others amounts to surrender of one's own self and denial of what it means to be human. Those who exhort humans to be unselfish aim to keep more talented and energetic people in servitude. This they do because they are parasites who wish to continue to benefit from the labours of the most inventive and productive members of society. In order to combat such exploitation by their intellectual and moral inferiors, the best members of the human race must cast off the burden of guilt they have unjustly been made to bear, because it is in fact the sole purpose of their lives to realize their egos to the fullest possible extent by pursuing their own interests in whatever way they choose. They might well make discoveries, produce machines or goods and devise methods and processes which turn out to be of universal use. In this sense, they will be benefactors to humankind, but the delivery of benefit to others is a by-product of their creativity, not their motivating force.

Randian heroes – exceptional individuals who possess drive, single-mindedness and clear-sightedness – see no reason why their activity should be regulated in any way by moral, philanthropic, economic, ecological or any other concerns expressed on behalf of inferior members of the human race. They have no doubts about the rightness of their actions because they are guided by an infallible systematic outlook and arrive at all their decisions by exercising their reason. Their conduct is unaffected by any sentiments, feeling for others, faith or other non-rational impulses, either because they have immunized themselves against them or because they have never experienced them. Liberated from the moral code obeyed by those who think that humans should, to some extent, live for, care for or take account of the interests of others, the Randian superman exists in a world beyond conventional understandings of good and evil. He demands the legal right to operate in an unregulated capitalist market, where he will be exempt from taxation. This right will enable him to find self-affirmation in two main ways. First, he will accumulate an unlimited amount of money, which is the new marker of aristocracy (*AS*: 90). Second, he will exercise complete control over the inferior beings whom he will put to work to realize his personal goals.

When Rand talks about the human personality and its needs, it is only the personality and needs of the beings she considers heroic in which she is interested. She makes this point, with magisterial condescension, in her introduction to the jubilee edition of *The Fountainhead* published in 1968. 'It does not matter', she writes here,

> that only a few in each generation will grasp and achieve the full reality of man's proper stature – and that the rest will betray it. It is those few that move the world and give life its meaning – and it is those few that I have always sought to address. The rest are no concern of mine; it is not me or *The Fountainhead* that they will betray; it is their own souls. (*F*: xiii)

At first sight, it seems odd that Rand, an atheist, should end such a programmatic statement about her work with the word 'souls'. After all, she incessantly and relentlessly abuses those philosophers or churchmen who posit the dualism of the human being and appeal to a spiritual dimension in their attempt to make people love their fellow humans. Is she using the term 'souls' vaguely, which would surely be inexcusable in one who thought of herself as a stern logician? And why should she see betrayal of one's 'soul' as the most grievous wound humans can inflict upon themselves? Perhaps the word seems more apt, though, if we regard Rand's writings as part of that grand quest to define a people's identity and destiny in which many a Russian writer or thinker had engaged. It serves to lift the reader to the other-worldly plane occupied by a prophet, and it is on that plane that Rand wishes to be judged. Nietzsche offered a model in this respect, but so did Dostoevsky, quite consciously.[1]

Dostoevsky's presence, along with that of contemporaries with whom Dostoevsky was constantly in dialogue, is strongly felt in Rand's prose fiction. For one thing, Dostoevsky provided the most powerful and influential models for the sort of novel Rand wrote, in which characters are reifications of ideas and an apocalyptic struggle between good and evil is taking place. He also articulated – with incomparably greater literary talent than Rand – values and key principles of an outlook which Rand considered it her life's mission to eradicate. His writings were replete with injunctions of the sort Rand deplored. He enjoined the headstrong, for instance, to reflect on their own responsibility for the ills of the world and to rein in their assertive egos. Acts of charity and humility, which were examples of great virtue in Dostoevsky's universe, were at best misguided in Rand's, whilst the Randian virtues of pride and love of money were indeed sins in Dostoevsky's eyes. At the same time, Dostoevsky's transgressors, who would cross existing moral boundaries without compunction, stand out, when viewed from Rand's vantage point, as heroic rule-breakers to be emulated rather than examples of monsters unleashed in a world without religious belief, as Dostoevsky had intended them to be.

Apocalyptic outcomes, as well as types of relationship between the individual and the collective and between extraordinary and ordinary humans, are treated in antithetical ways in Dostoevsky's and Rand's novels. From Rand's point of view, the scenes of economic breakdown, social anarchy and political collapse in the dénouement of *Atlas Shrugged* represent a triumph for her heroes. Seen through a Dostoevskian lens, on the other hand, they look much like those in Raskol'nikov nightmare in the epilogue of *Crime and Punishment*. This revelatory dream occurs at the point in the novel where Raskol'nikov, imprisoned in a Siberian penal settlement, is beginning to understand the true import of his attempt to prove that, as an exceptional being, he could cross conventional moral boundaries with impunity. In his nightmare, almost everyone in Europe is infected with a pestilence spreading from the heart of Asia. Convinced of their own infallibility, individuals and whole communities start to kill one another, precipitating war, fire and famine, until only a few men and women remain. These survivors were 'the pure and the chosen, those destined to begin a new race of people and a new life, to renew and purify the earth'.[2]

In articulating her extreme individualistic and anti-egalitarian conception of America's identity and mission, Rand drew heavily on, engaged with, and in some respects reversed ideas that had currency among the intelligentsia of the nation in which she had been formed. These ideas concerned the aesthetic, moral, metaphysical, political, economic and geopolitical questions that had preoccupied members of the Russian intelligentsia at both ends of the political spectrum from the mid-nineteenth century onwards. In discussing them, moreover, Rand proceeded in ways characteristic of that intelligentsia, especially its radical wing. She adopted a tone of moral righteousness. She preached. She was intolerant. She abused her opponents. She was uncompromising and despised those who sought middle ground. Reasoning on any subject, for her, entailed selection of the correct element in a binary opposition. She sought the certainties that a supposedly scientific approach to intellectual enquiry seemed to promise. She was an ideological thinker who wished to integrate all knowledge and views on any subject into a logically consistent whole. Her choice of the novel as the vehicle for debate about the questions that interested her was also part of a Russian legacy. Offered to an anglophone readership in a different cultural, intellectual, political and economic context, Rand's literary formula had the appearance of great originality and made a major contribution to right-wing political thought in the Western world. Its deepest source, though, was the well of ideas imbibed and habits learned from the Russian intelligentsia, of which she always remained, throughout more than fifty years in emigration, a rather typical representative.

NOTES

Introduction

1   Lisa Duggan, *Mean Girl: Ayn Rand and the Culture of Greed* (Oakland: University of California Press, 2019), 89. Duggan locates her book in the field of American cultural studies and explains the breadth of and reasons for the appeal of Rand's fiction.

2   For a recent discussion of Rand's influence in the United States, especially her influence on Greenspan, see Adam Weiner, *How Bad Writing Destroyed the World: Ayn Rand and the Literary Origins of the Financial Crisis* (New York, etc.: Bloomsbury Academic, 2016). On the 'Collective' and Rand's life and work more generally, see the three most authoritative biographies of her: Barbara Branden, *The Passion of Ayn Rand* (New York: Anchor Books, 1987); Anne C. Heller, *Ayn Rand and the World She Made* (New York, etc.: Nan A. Talese, 2009); and Jennifer Burns, *Goddess of the Market: Ayn Rand and the American Right* (Oxford: Oxford University Press, 2009). Branden's biography is a primary source, inasmuch as its author was on intimate terms with Rand for almost twenty years and a core member of her inner circle.

3   Firmin DeBrabander, 'How Ayn Rand's "Elitism" Lives on in the Trump Administration', *The Conversation*, 4 April 2017, https://theconversation.com/how-ayn-rands-elitism-lives-on-in-the-trump-administration-74739 (accessed 13.11.2020).

4   Jonathan Chait, 'Paul Ryan and the Republican Vision', *The New Republic*, 11 March 2010, https://newrepublic.com/article/73669/paul-ryan-and-the-republican-vision (accessed 13.11.2020).

5   Branden, *The Passion of Ayn Rand*, 421–2.

6   Duggan, *Mean Girl*, 78, 88.

7   For comment on Rand's influence on elements of the modern British Conservative Party, see George Monbiot, 'How Ayn Rand Became the New Right's Version of Marx', *The Guardian*, 5 March 2012, https://www.theguardian.com/commentisfree/2012/mar/05/new-right-ayn-rand-marx; Jonathan Freedland, 'The New Age of Ayn Rand: How She Won over Trump and Silicon Valley', *The Guardian*, 10 April 2017, https://www.theguardian.com/books/2017/apr/10/new-age-ayn-rand-conquered-trump-white-house-silicon-valley; Alastair Benn, 'Why

Notes

Do Tories Love Ayn Rand?', https://blogs.spectator.co.uk/2018/05/why-do-tories-love-ayn-rand/; and Rachel Sylvester, 'Both Sides Now: Inside the Rise of Sajid Javid', *Prospect*, 27 January 2019, https://www.prospectmagazine.co.uk/politics/both-sides-now-inside-the-rise-of-sajid-javid (all accessed 13.11.2020).

8   The ARI site is at https://aynrand.org/ (accessed 12.11.2020).
9   'Basic Principles of Literature', in Rand, *The Romantic Manifesto: A Philosophy of Literature*, 2nd revised edn (New York: Signet, 1975), 73 (Rand's italics).
10   Burns, *Goddess of the Market*, 2.
11   For an extended list of examples, see the epilogue in Branden, *The Passion of Ayn Rand*, 407–22.
12   Ed Kilgore, 'Donald Trump's Role Model Is an Ayn Rand Character', *The Intelligencer*, 12 April 2016, https://nymag.com/intelligencer/2016/04/trumps-role-model-is-an-ayn-rand-character.html (accessed 29.10.2020).
13   Chait, 'Paul Ryan and the Republican Vision'.
14   Burns, *Goddess of the Market*, 4.
15   Burns, *Goddess of the Market*, 170–2.
16   Duggan, *Mean Girl*, 4–5.
17   Burns, *Goddess of the Market*, 72–3. Keynes's *General Theory of Employment, Interest and Money* was published in 1936.
18   *Journals of Ayn Rand*, ed. David Harriman, with a foreword by Leonard Peikoff (New York: Plume, 1999), 356.
19   See Samuel P. Huntington, *The Clash of Civilizations and the Remaking of World Order* (New York: Simon and Schuster, 1996).
20   Heller, *Ayn Rand*, 51.
21   Rand's published non-fictional writings include collections whose titles capture salient features of her outlook, such as *The Virtue of Selfishness: A New Concept of Egoism* (New York: New American Library, 1964), *Capitalism: The Unknown Ideal* (New York: Signet, 1967) and *The Romantic Manifesto: A Philosophy of Literature*.
22   I have written separately about this novel: see Derek Offord, 'Ayn Rand's *Fountainhead* and Its Russian Antecedents', *Modern Language Review* 115, no. 4 (October 2020), 763–90.
23   *Journals of Ayn Rand*, 269.

Chapter 1

1   On Rand's years at the Stoiunina school, see Heller, *Ayn Rand*, 17–21.
2   On Rand's friendship with Ol'ga Nabokova, see Heller, *Ayn Rand*, 26–7. For a comparison of the careers of Vladimir Nabokov and Rand

as writers in the Russian diaspora, see D. Barton Johnson, 'Strange Bedfellows: Ayn Rand and Vladimir Nabokov', *Journal of Ayn Rand Studies* 2, no. 1 (Fall 2000), 47–67.

3   Thanks to the Bolsheviks, women were now admitted to higher education institutions and tuition was free, as noted by Duggan, *Mean Girl*, 18–19.

4   Heller, *Ayn Rand*, 18–21.

5   Heller, *Ayn Rand*, 6–8.

6   Branden, *The Passion of Ayn Rand*, 7, 194, 172.

7   The Collective, incidentally, was made up almost entirely of people of Russian-Jewish background who were relatives and friends of Nathaniel Branden and his Canadian wife Barbara (*née* Weidman, Rand's first major biographer) and their partners. This point is made by Duggan, *Mean Girl*, 57.

8   See Branden, *The Passion of Ayn Rand*, xi, 269–71.

9   Benjamin Nathans, *Beyond the Pale: The Jewish Encounter with Late Imperial Russia* (Berkeley, Los Angeles and London: University of California Press, 2002), 285–92, 246.

10   James P. Scanlan, *Dostoevsky the Thinker* (Ithaca and London: Cornell University Press, 2002), 209–11.

11   Nathans, *Beyond the Pale*, 311, 361–2.

12   Nathans, *Beyond the Pale*, 10, 334–9, 374, 377, 378.

13   Nathans, *Beyond the Pale*, 87, 126–30.

14   Nathans, *Beyond the Pale*, 165–8.

15   Branden, *The Passion of Ayn Rand*, 6 n.

16   Branden, *The Passion of Ayn Rand*, 4–6.

17   Branden, *The Passion of Ayn Rand*, 6.

18   Branden, *The Passion of Ayn Rand*, 34, 72.

19   Branden, *The Passion of Ayn Rand*, 286.

20   Heller, *Ayn Rand*, 31–2.

21   For a broad survey of the Symbolists, see D. S. Mirsky, *A History of Russian Literature*, ed. and abridged by Francis J. Whitfield (London: Routledge and Kegan Paul, 1968), 430–84.

22   On the World of Art and Silver-Age painting, see Camilla Grey, *The Russian Experiment in Art: 1863–1922* (New York: Harry N. Abrams, 1970).

23   I have drawn in this paragraph on Ruth Coates, 'Religious Renaissance in the Silver Age', in William Leatherbarrow and Derek Offord (eds), *A History of Russian Thought* (Cambridge: Cambridge University Press, 2010), 169–93, and Mirsky, *A History of Russian Literature*, 418–26.

24   Judith Deutsch Kornblatt, 'Eschatology and Hope in Silver Age Thought', in *A History of Russian Philosophy, 1830–1930: Faith, Reason, and the Defense of Human Dignity*, ed. G. M. Hamburg and Randall A.

Poole (Cambridge: Cambridge University Press, 2010), 285–301 (here p. 287).

25 *The Devils* is also translated as *The Possessed*. On apocalyptic imagery in these two novels, see William J. Leatherbarrow, *Fedor Dostoevsky* (Boston: Twayne Publishers, 1981), 98–103 and 127–9.

26 'Introduction', in Rand, *The Romantic Manifesto*, vi (Rand's italics).

27 'Art and Cognition', in Rand, *The Romantic Manifesto*, 39, 68, 55 (Rand's italics).

28 Heller, *Ayn Rand*, 339, 44, 299.

29 Argounova is the form of the Russian surname used by Rand in the novel; the transliteration of this name according to the system used in this book would be Argunova.

30 See Chris Matthew Sciabarra, *Ayn Rand: The Russian Radical* (University Park: Pennsylvania University Press, 1995; 2nd augmented edn 2013 (digital)). This is the major study of Rand's engagement with the philosophy of the Russian Silver Age (i.e. the early twentieth century), of which Rand, Sciabarra argues, was a product. Sciabarra characterizes Rand as a thinker in the radical libertarian tradition and defines her philosophy, as I do, as a response to her Russian past. Her Russianness, he finds, is manifested in her penchant for dialectical thinking and her quest for wholeness, a sort of Hegelian synthesis which would overcome the dualism that allegedly perplexed Russian thinkers. Rand also belonged within the Russian literary and philosophic tradition, Sciabarra argues, by virtue of her predilection for grand generalizations and her commitment to the realization of her ideals.

31 Branden, *The Passion of Ayn Rand*, 24, 376.

32 Heller, *Ayn Rand*, 41–2. On Russians' engagement with Nietzsche in the Silver Age, see Bernice Glatzer Rosenthal (ed.), *Nietzsche in Russia* (Princeton: Princeton University Press, 1986), and Coates, 'Religious Renaissance in the Silver Age', 187–9.

33 Nietzsche's influence on Rand is particularly emphasized by Burns, *Goddess of the Market*: see pp. 22, 25–6, 28, 30, 41–3, 51, and n. 4 on pp. 303–4.

34 'Basic Principles of Literature', in Rand, *The Romantic Manifesto*, 77, 80; 'Art and Sense of Life', ibid., 33.

35 'What Is Romanticism?', ibid., 99.

36 'The Russian Idea' (*Russkaia ideia*) is the title of one of the best-known books by the above-mentioned Berdiaev.

37 This misrepresentation of the true significance of Dostoevsky for Rand is also evident in the account of Branden, who asserts that Rand admired Dostoevsky 'for more narrowly literary and technical reasons than she had liked Schiller' (Branden, *The Passion of Ayn Rand*, 45).

38   'Art and Sense of Life', in Rand, *The Romantic Manifesto*, 33.
39   As for Dostoevsky's contemporary Tolstoy, with whose work Rand was
     of course also familiar, Rand considered his 'philosophy' and 'sense of
     life' 'not merely mistaken, but evil', and *Anna Karenina*, she thought,
     was 'the most evil book in serious literature' ('Art and Sense of Life', in
     Rand, *The Romantic Manifesto*, 34; 'What Is Romanticism?', ibid., 109).
     At the same time, it has been suggested to me by an anonymous reader,
     there is perhaps something Tolstoyan about the relish with which Rand
     accepted the formation of a cult around her.
40   See the useful 'Essay on Sources' in Burns, *Goddess of the Market*,
     291–3.
41   Burns, *Goddess of the Market*, 304, nn. 13 and 14, and 305, n. 19,
     respectively.
42   *Journals of Ayn Rand*, 23. Harriman's generous remarks on Rand's
     positive side are immediately followed by a passage in the notebooks
     which perfectly illustrates Rand's negative side: 'Show that *humanity is
     petty*', she jots. 'That it's small. That it's dumb, with the heavy, hopeless
     stupidity of a man born feeble-minded', and so forth (ibid., 23–4;
     Rand's italics)!
43   Of the many scholarly works on Chernyshevsky, Irina Paperno's
     Chernyshevsky and the Age of Realism: A Study in the Semiotics of Behavior
     (Stanford: Stanford University Press, 1988) offers the most probing
     examination of the influence of Chernyshevsky's novel and of the ways in
     which the author's life, ideas and preoccupations are reflected in it.
44   *Journals of Ayn Rand*, 38.

Chapter 2

1   The phrase is the title of a review written by the influential radical
    literary critic Nikolai Dobroliubov of a play by Aleksandr Ostrovsky.
2   On these and other nineteenth-century Russian journals, see Deborah
    Martinsen (ed.), *Literary Journals in Imperial Russia* (Cambridge:
    Cambridge University Press, 1997).
3   S. I. Ozhegov, *Slovar' russkogo iazyka*, 20th edn (Moscow: Russkii
    iazyk, 1988).
4   The term is nowadays applied retrospectively to figures who flourished
    as far back as the 1840s. There is a large literature on the intelligentsia
    broadly understood in this way: see especially Isaiah Berlin, *Russian
    Thinkers*, ed. Henry Hardy and Aileen Kelly, 2nd revised edn (London:
    Penguin, 2008).
5   Nathans, *Beyond the Pale*, 10.

Notes

6   See, e.g., the *Oxford English Dictionary*, 2nd edn: VII, 1070.

7   'Art and Sense of Life', in Rand, *The Romantic Manifesto*, 29.

8   Branden, *The Passion of Ayn Rand*, 243.

9   Heller, *Ayn Rand*, 18.

10   Heller, *Ayn Rand*, 121.

11   On the beginnings of this affair, see Branden, *The Passion of Ayn Rand*, 257–64; Heller, *Ayn Rand*, 255–9; Burns, *Goddess of the Market*, 155–7.

12   *Journals of Ayn Rand*, 128, 135, 348–9, 693.

13   *Journals of Ayn Rand*, 65.

14   *Istoricheskie pis'ma*, in P. L. Lavrov, *Izbrannye sochineniia na sotsial'no-politicheskie temy*, 4 vols published (Moscow: Izdatel'stvo vsesoiuznogo obshchestva politkatorzhan i ssyl'no-poselentsev, 1934–5); see especially Lavrov's fourth 'letter' in vol. I, 216–26.

15   *Journals of Ayn Rand*, 95.

16   On 'unmercenariness' among the intelligentsia, see Derek Offord, 'Worshipping the Golden Calf: The Intelligentsia's Conception of the Bourgeois World in the Age of Nicholas', in Joe Andrew, Derek Offord and Robert Reid (eds), *Turgenev and Russian Culture: Essays to Honour Richard Peace* (Amsterdam and New York: Rodopi, 2008), 237–57.

17   *The Oxford English Dictionary* cites examples of the expression dating from 1457, c. 1470, 1546 and 1588 (https://www.oed.com/, accessed 05.04.2020), i.e. before the voyage of the Mayflower that took Puritans to New England in 1620 and even before the discovery of the Americas by Christopher Columbus in 1492.

18   Branden, *The Passion of Ayn Rand*, 35.

19   Branden, *The Passion of Ayn Rand*, 52. See also her television interview with James McConnell in 1961: search for 'Videos of James McConnell interview of Ayn Rand 1961'.

20   'Esteticheskie otnosheniia iskusstva k deistvitel'nosti', in N. G. Chernyshevsky, *Polnoe sobranie sochinenii*, 16 vols (Moscow: Gosudarstvennoe izdatel'stvo khudozhestvennoi literatury, 1939–53; hereafter Chernyshevsky, *PSS*), II, 5–92.

21   'Razrushenie estetiki', in D. I. Pisarev, *Sochineniia*, 4 vols (Moscow: Gosudarstvennoe izdatel'stvo khudozhestvennoi literatury, 1955–6), III, 418–35.

22   For a useful overview of the development of the tradition of radical Russian criticism, see Charles A. Moser, *Esthetics as Nightmare: Russian Literary Theory, 1855–1870* (Princeton: Princeton University Press, 1989). On Russian radical thought more generally in this period, see Richard Peace, 'Nihilism', in Leatherbarrow and Offord (eds), *A History of Russian Thought*, 116–40.

23 On this type, see Rufus W. Matthewson, *The Positive Hero in Russian Literature* (New York: Columbia University Press, 1958; revised edn, Stanford University Press, 1975).

24 Weiner, *How Bad Writing Destroyed the World*.

25 On Rand's disdain for Plato, see, e.g., Branden, *The Passion of Ayn Rand*, 42; Heller, *Ayn Rand*, 41.

Chapter 3

1   See Rand's foreword to *We the Living*, with an introduction by Leonard Peikoff (London: Penguin, 2009), xv, xiii.

2   Heller, *Ayn Rand*, 277.

3   *Besy*, Part 2, chapter 7, in F. M. Dostoevskii, *Polnoe sobranie sochinenii*, 30 vols (Leningrad: Nauka, 1972–90; hereafter Dostoevsky, *PSS*), X, 311.

4   *Besy*, Part 2, chapter 8, in Dostoevskii, *PSS*, X, 322.

5   *Brat'ia Karamazovy*, Book 5, chapter 5, in Dostoevskii, *PSS*, XIV, 224–41.

6   Weiner, *How Bad Writing Destroyed the World*, 193. On the literary relationship between Zamiatin and Rand, see also Zina Gimpelevich, "'We' and 'I' in Zamyatin's *We* and Rand's *Anthem*', *Germano-Slavica* 10, no. 1 (1997), 13–23, and Peter Saint-Andre, 'Zamyatin and Rand', *Journal of Ayn Rand Studies* 4, no. 2 (2003), 285–304. The similarity of *Anthem* to *We* is acknowledged by Barbara Branden, but more to point up the difference between the two works and Rand's supposed originality than to underline their resemblance (Branden, *The Passion of Ayn Rand*, 143).

7   Zamiatin's novel was finally published in Soviet Russia in 1988, at the time of *perestroika*.

8   *Kto vinovat?*, in A. I. Gertsen [Herzen], *Sobranie sochinenii*, 30 vols (Moscow: Izdatel'stvo Akademii nauk SSSR, 1954–65), IV, 9–209.

9   *Journals of Ayn Rand*, 345.

10 Heller, *Ayn Rand*, 130–4; Burns, *Goddess of the Market*, 53–7.

11 Burns, *Goddess of the Market*, 61.

12 Regarding the use of the word 'man' in this quotation, Rand invariably prefers this gendered noun to 'human being' or 'humans' whenever she generalizes about humankind. This usage was of course commonplace in her day. However, she really does seem on the whole to regard men as the driving force in human affairs and to grant women only occasional honorary status in men's important associations.

13 A. F. Pisemky, *Vzbalamuchennoe more*; N. S. Leskov, *Nekuda*; Dostoevsky, *Besy*. On this variety of the novel of ideas in Russia, see Charles A. Moser, *Antinihilism in the Russian Novel of the 1860's* (The Hague: Mouton, 1964).

Notes

14   On Sleptsov's novella, see Derek Offord, 'Literature and Ideas in Russia after the Crimean War: The "Plebeian" Writers', in Richard Freeborn and Jane Grayson (eds), *Ideology in Russian Literature* (Basingstoke and London: Macmillan, 1990), 71–4. Kravchinsky wrote under the pen name Stepniak. On novels of this type, see Richard Freeborn, *The Russian Revolutionary Novel: Turgenev to Pasternak* (Cambridge: Cambridge University Press, 1983).

15   *Journals of Ayn Rand*, 25.

16   *Chto delat'?*, in Chernyshevsky, *PSS*, XI, 277–9.

17   At the time when Chernyshevsky wrote *What Is to Be Done?*, aluminium could only be extracted in small quantities and at great expense from the ores in which it occurs, and it was therefore not available for large-scale use. Rand's first fictional heroine, Kira Argounova, also dreams of building houses of glass and steel and a bridge of aluminium (*WL*, 35).

18   *Chto delat'?*, in Chernyshevsky, *PSS*, XI, 199–202, 207.

19   'Krakh II Internatsionala', in V. I. Lenin, *Polnoe sobranie sochinenii*, 5th edn, 55 vols (Moscow: Institut Marksizma-Leninizma, 1958–65), XXVI, 218.

20   *Journals of Ayn Rand*, 390.

21   *Ottsy i deti*, in Turgenev, *Polnoe sobranie sochinenii i pisem,* 28 vols (Moscow and Leningrad: Izdatel'stvo Akademii nauk SSSR, 1961–8), VIII, 243.

22   Harold Laski, a leading figure in the early post-war British Left and chairman of the British Labour Party in 1945–6, who gave a lecture that Rand attended in New York in 1937 and whom she detested, served as a model for her arch-villain Ellsworth Toohey in *The Fountainhead*: see *Journals of Ayn Rand*, 113–15.

23   Burns, *Goddess of the Market*, 61–5. This document, which is preserved among personal papers in the Ayn Rand Archives, has not been published, but Burns was given access to it. Rand's slogan, incidentally, is written in capital letters, like that of Marx and Engels.

24   Rand, *Capitalism: The Unknown Ideal*, 40–62.

25   Katerina Clark, *The Soviet Novel: History as Ritual*, 3rd edn (Bloomington and Indianapolis: Indiana University Press, 2000), 9.

26   Geoffrey Hosking, *A History of the Soviet Union* (London: Fontana, 1985), 222.

27   See David Gillespie, 'Nikolai Alekseevich Ostrovskii 1904–1936', in *Reference Guide to Russian Literature*, 608–9.

28   See Roger Cockrell, 'Dmitrii Andreevich Furmanov 1891–1926', in *Reference Guide to Russian Literature*, 308–9, and 'Chapaev', ibid., 309–10; see also Clark, *The Soviet Novel*, 84–8.

29   On the relationship of *The Mother* to *What Is to Be Done?*, see Johnson
       'Strange Bedfellows', 53–4. On the martyr in Socialist Realist fiction, see
       Clark, *The Soviet Novel*, 72–4.
30   On this work (*Kliatva*), see Cockrell, 'Fedor Vasil'evich Gladkov
       1883–1958', in *Reference Guide to Russian Literature*, 327–8.
31   See Cockrell, 'Fedor Vasil'evich Gladkov 1883–1958', 327.
32   The comparison is also made by Weiner, *How Bad Writing Destroyed
       the World*, 206.
33   Clark, *The Soviet Novel*, xi.
34   Clark, *The Soviet Novel*, 36–41.
35   *Journals of Ayn Rand*, 355–67.
36   Johnson, 'Strange Bedfellows', 64.

Chapter 4

1   For an overview of Dostoevsky's objections to Chernyshevsky's world-
       outlook, see Derek Offord, 'Dostoyevsky and Chernyshevsky', *The
       Slavonic and East European Review* 57, no. 4 (October 1979), 509–30.
2   *Zimnie zametki o letnikh vpechatleniiakh*, in Dostoevsky, *PSS*, V, 79.
3   'What Is Romanticism?', in Rand, *The Romantic Manifesto*, 108.
4   The quotation is in capitals in the inscription.
5   *Cambridge Dictionary* at https://dictionary.cambridge.org/dictionary/
       english/empathy (accessed 14.11.2020).
6   'Bazarov', in Pisarev, *Sochineniia*, II, 7–50 (here pp. 20–1).
7   *Chto delat'?* in Chernyshevsky, *PSS*, XI, 197, 210.
8   *Prestuplenie i nakazanie*, in Dostoevsky, *PSS*, VI, 199–201
       (Dostoevsky's italics).
9   *Prestuplenie i nakazanie*, in Dostoevsky, *PSS*, VI, 200.
10   *Journals of Ayn Rand*, 35, 393.
11   *Second-hand Lives* was Rand's working title for *The Fountainhead* right
       up to the point when the publisher who accepted the book suggested
       it be changed, on the grounds that it drew attention to her negative
       characters rather than the positive aspect of her philosophy of egoism
       (Branden, *The Passion of Ayn Rand*, 175).
12   See *Brat'ia Karamazovy*, in Dostoevsky, *PSS*, XIV, 64–5.
13   On Rand's drug-taking, see Branden, *The Passion of Ayn Rand*, 173–4 n.
14   *Journals of Ayn Rand*, 24.
15   That is, 'Der Mensch ist was er isst': see Peace, 'Nihilism', 128–9.
16   'Antropologicheskii printsip v filosofii', in Chernyshevsky, *PSS*, VII, 264.
17   'Basic Principles of Literature', in Rand, *The Romantic Manifesto*, 72.
18   cf. Descartes: 'Cogito ergo sum' (I think, therefore I am).

Notes

19 *Zapiski iz podpol'ia*, in Dostoevsky, *PSS*, V, 115, 118–19.

20 The phenomenon we call the will, Chernyshevsky argued in an essay of 1860, was just a 'link in a series of phenomena and factors united by a causal connection' ('Antropologicheskii printsip v filosofii', in Chernyshevsky, *PSS*, VII, 261).

Chapter 5

1 Friedrich Engels, *Herr Eugen Dühring's Revolution in Science*, commonly known as the *Anti-Dühring* (Moscow: Progress Publishers, 1947), online version at https://www.marxists.org/archive/marx/works/download/pdf/anti_duhring.pdf (accessed 12.11.2020), 177.

2 *Zapiski iz podpol'ia*, in Dostoevsky, *PSS*, V, 110–17.

3 Branden, *The Passion of Ayn Rand*, 115.

4 Branden, *The Passion of Ayn Rand*, 114. The words in question were expunged in a new edition of *We the Living* published in 1959.

5 See also *Journals of Ayn Rand*, 96.

6 Burns, *Goddess of the Market*, 212.

7 Revelations, 21:24 and 27 (italics in the source).

8 *Journals of Ayn Rand*, 236.

9 Although, as Heller points out, the requirement that Rand's diffident young lover Branden dominate her does make one wonder quite who was in control of whom: Heller, *Ayn Rand*, 259.

10 Branden, *The Passion of Ayn Rand*, 398.

11 Burns, *Goddess of the Market*, 45.

12 For such an attempt, see Mimi Reisel Gladstein, 'Ayn Rand and Feminism: An Unlikely Alliance', *College English* 39, no. 6 (February 1978), 680–5.

13 Branden, *The Passion of Ayn Rand*, 17, 189 (my italics; DO), 412.

14 *Journals of Ayn Rand*, 74.

15 *Journals of Ayn Rand*, 549.

16 Heller, *Ayn Rand*, 29.

17 Senator Mike Lee of Utah, in a tweet of 8 October 2020.

18 George Monbiot, 'There is a civil war in capitalism, and we're the collateral damage', *The Guardian*, Wednesday, 25 November 2020, *Journal*, 1. Monbiot cites *Atlas Shrugged*, along with *The Constitution of Liberty* (1960) by Friedrich Hayek, as the sources of the 'justifying ideology' of warlord capitalism. It is argued by Weiner that the deregulation carried out by Rand's protégé Greenspan in the 1990s and early 2000s, in the belief that the free market should be allowed to regulate itself, contributed significantly to the global financial crisis of 2007–8: Weiner, *How Bad Writing Destroyed the World*, 12–16. See also Duggan, *Mean Girl*, 86–9.

Chapter 6

1   'Lettre première', in P. N. Chaadaev, *Polnoe sobranie sochinenii i izbrannye pis'ma*, 2 vols (Moscow: Izdatel'stvo nauka, 1991), I, 86–106.

2   *Pis'ma iz Frantsii i Italii*, in Gertsen, *Sobranie sochinenii*, V, 81, 212.

3   *Brat'ia Karamazovy*, in Dostoevsky, *PSS*, XIV, 210.

4   Alexis de Tocqueville, *De la démocratie en Amérique*.

5   Gertsen, *Sobranie sochinenii*, V, 432.

6   *Besy*, in Dostoevsky, *PSS*, X, 111–12.

7   Korolenko attended the universal exhibition held in Chicago (the Chicago World's Fair) in 1893. He presented his unfavourable impressions of America's political and economic life in a novella, *Speechless* (*Bez iazyka*, 1895): see the entry on Korolenko by Radha Balasubramanian in *Reference Guide to Russian Literature*, 465–6. Gorky left a darker reflection on life in New York, 'The City of the Yellow Devil' (*Gorod zheltogo d'iavola*, 1906). Gorky indicts the voracious appetite for profit (symbolized by accumulation of gold, the 'yellow devil' to which the title of his sketch refers) and dwells on the dehumanizing effect of life in this polluted city of stone, glass and iron. The sketch is available online at http://az.lib.ru/g/gorxkij_m/text_1906_gorod_zheltogo_diavola.shtml (accessed 10.05.2020).

8   For a readable translation of Mayakovsky's travelogue and a useful introduction to it, see Vladimir Mayakovsky, *My Discovery of America*, trans. Neil Cornwell (London: Hesperus, Modern Voices series, 2005). Mayakovsky's work also included sketches of Cuba and Mexico, which he visited during the same trip.

9   See the notes in vol. VII of Vladimir Mayakovsky, *Polnoe sobranie sochinenii*, 13 vols (Gosudarstvennoe izdatel'stvo khudozhestvennoi literatury, 1955–61), available online at http://az.lib.ru/m/majakowskij_w_w/text_0530.shtml (accessed 02.05.2020). Prior to publication of *My Discovery of America*, Mayakovsky spoke about his impressions of America at various literary evenings, e.g., in Moscow on 6 and 19 December 1925.

10   Mayakovsky, *My Discovery of America*, 103.

11   Mayakovsky, *My Discovery of America*, 63–4.

12   Mayakovsky, *My Discovery of America*, 105–6.

13   Branden, *The Passion of Ayn Rand*, 23.

14   See also *Journals of Ayn Rand*, 349.

15   The comparison of the Socialist Realist hero with the American frontiersman is made by Clark, *The Soviet Novel*, 73.

16   See *Brat'ia Karamazovy*, in Dostoevsky, *PSS*, XIV, 25.

Notes

17 Rand's testimony is reproduced in *Journals of Ayn Rand*, 371–81. See also Heller, *Ayn Rand*, 200–6, 245–7, and Burns, *Goddess of the Market*, 124–5.

18 'Introduction', in Rand, *The Romantic Manifesto*, vii, and 'Basic Principles of Literature', ibid., 90.

19 For a recent discussion of narratives about American identity and Rand's place in them, see George Packer, 'How America Fractured into Four Parts', *The Atlantic*, July/August 2021. Rand belongs, of course, in the traditionalist and anti-communist narrative that Packer defines as 'Free America', but she also has strong appeal, I think, to those who are drawn to the more contemporary narrative about 'Real America' that Packer identifies and which he associates with Donald Trump.

20 *Journals of Ayn Rand*, 357 (Rand's italics).

Conclusion

1 As suggested by the title of the last volume of Joseph Frank's five-volume literary biography *Dostoevsky: The Mantle of the Prophet, 1871–1881* (Princeton: Princeton University Press, 2002).

2 *Prestuplenie i nakazanie*, in Dostoevsky, *PSS*, VI, 419–20. I have used here the translation by Oliver Ready in Fyodor Dostoyevsky, *Crime and Punishment* (London: Penguin Random House UK, 2014), 654–5.

SELECTED BIBLIOGRAPHY

ARI official website of the Ayn Rand Institute https://www.aynrand.org.

Balasubramanian, Radha, 'Vladimir Galaktionovich Korolenko 1853–1921', in *Reference Guide to Russian Literature*, ed. Neil Cornwell (Chicago: Fitzroy Dearborn, 1998), 465–6.

Benn, Alastair, 'Why Do Tories Love Ayn Rand?' https://blogs.spectator. co.uk/2018/05/why-do-tories-love-ayn-rand/.

Berlin, Isaiah, *Russian Thinkers*, ed. Henry Hardy and Aileen Kelly, 2nd revised edn (London: Penguin, 2008).

Branden, Barbara, *The Passion of Ayn Rand* (New York: Anchor Books, 1987).

Burns, Jennifer, *Goddess of the Market: Ayn Rand and the American Right* (Oxford: Oxford University Press, 2009).

Chaadaev, P. N., *Polnoe sobranie sochinenii i izbrannye pis'ma*, 2 vols (Moscow: Izdatel'stvo nauka, 1991).

Chait, Jonathan, 'Paul Ryan and the Republican Vision', *The New Republic*, 11 March 2010. https://newrepublic.com/article/73669/paul-ryan-and-the-republican-vision.

Chernyshevsky, N. G., *Polnoe sobranie sochinenii*, 16 vols (Moscow: Gosudarstvennoe izdatel'stvo khudozhestvennoi literatury, 1939–53).

Clark, Katerina, *The Soviet Novel: History as Ritual*, 3rd edn (Bloomington and Indianapolis: Indiana University Press, 2000).

Coates, Ruth, 'Religious Renaissance in the Silver Age', in *A History of Russian Thought*, ed. William Leatherbarrow and Derek Offord (Cambridge: Cambridge University Press, 2010), 169–93.

Cockrell, Roger, 'Chapaev', in *Reference Guide to Russian Literature*, ed. Neil Cornwell (Chicago: Fitzroy Dearborn, 1998), 309–10.

Cockrell, Roger, 'Dmitrii Andreevich Furmanov 1891–1926', in *Reference Guide to Russian Literature*, ed. Neil Cornwell (Chicago: Fitzroy Dearborn, 1998), 308–9.

Cockrell, Roger, 'Fedor Vasil'evich Gladkov 1883–1958', in *Reference Guide to Russian Literature*, ed. Neil Cornwell (Chicago: Fitzroy Dearborn, 1998), 327–8.

De Brabander, Firmin, 'How Ayn Rand's "Elitism" Lives on in the Trump Administration', *The Conversation*, 4 April 2017. https://

theconversation.com/how-ayn-rands-elitism-lives-on-in-the-trump-administration-74739.

Dostoevsky, F. M., *Polnoe sobranie sochinenii*, 30 vols (Leningrad: Nauka, 1972–90).

Duggan, Lisa, *Mean Girl: Ayn Rand and the Culture of Greed* (Oakland: University of California Press, 2019).

Engels, Friedrich, *Herr Eugen Dühring's Revolution in Science* (Moscow: Progress Publishers, 1947). https://www.marxists.org/archive/marx/works/download/pdf/anti_duhring.pdf.

Frank, Joseph, *Dostoevsky: The Mantle of the Prophet, 1871–1881* (Princeton: Princeton University Press, 2002).

Freeborn, Richard, *The Russian Revolutionary Novel: Turgenev to Pasternak* (Cambridge: Cambridge University Press, 1983).

Freedland, Jonathan, 'The New Age of Ayn Rand: How She Won over Trump and Silicon Valley', *The Guardian*, 10 April 2017. https://www.theguardian.com/books/2017/apr/10/new-age-ayn-rand-conquered-trump-white-house-silicon-valley.

Gertsen [Herzen], A. I., *Sobranie sochinenii*, 30 vols (Moscow: Izdatel'stvo Akademii nauk SSSR, 1954–65).

Gillespie, David, 'Nikolai Alekseevich Ostrovskii 1904–1936', in *Reference Guide to Russian Literature*, ed. Neil Cornwell (Chicago: Fitzroy Dearborn, 1998), 608–9.

Gimpelevich, Zina, '"We" and "I" in Zamyatin's *We* and Rand's *Anthem*', *Germano-Slavica* 10, no. 1 (1997), 13–23.

Gladstein, Mimi Reisel, 'Ayn Rand and Feminism: An Unlikely Alliance', *College English* 39, no. 6 (February 1978), 680–5.

Grey, Camilla, *The Russian Experiment in Art: 1863–1922* (New York: Harry N. Abrams, 1970).

Heller, Anne C., *Ayn Rand and the World She Made* (New York, etc.: Nan A. Talese, 2009).

Hosking, Geoffrey, *A History of the Soviet Union* (London: Fontana, 1985).

Huntington, Samuel P., *The Clash of Civilizations and the Remaking of World Order* (New York: Simon and Schuster, 1996).

Johnson, D. Barton, 'Strange Bedfellows: Ayn Rand and Vladimir Nabokov', *Journal of Ayn Rand Studies* 2, no. 1 (Fall 2000), 47–67.

Kilgore, Ed, 'Donald Trump's Role Model Is an Ayn Rand Character', *The Intelligencer*, 12 April 2016. https://nymag.com/intelligencer/2016/04/trumps-role-model-is-an-ayn-rand-character.html.

Kornblatt, Judith Deutsch, 'Eschatology and Hope in Silver Age Thought', in *A History of Russian Philosophy, 1830–1930: Faith, Reason, and the Defense of Human Dignity*, ed. G. M. Hamburg and Randall A. Poole (Cambridge: Cambridge University Press, 2010), 285–301.

Lavrov, P. L., *Izbrannye sochineniia na sotsial'no-politicheskie temy*, 4 vols published (Moscow: Izdatel'stvo vsesoiuznogo obshchestva politkatorzhan i ssyl'no-poselentsev, 1934–35).

Leatherbarrow, William J., *Fedor Dostoevsky* (Boston: Twayne Publishers, 1981).

Lenin, *Polnoe sobranie sochinenii*, 5th edn, 55 vols (Moscow: Institut Marksizma-Leninizma, 1958–65).

Martinsen, Deborah (ed.), *Literary Journals in Imperial Russia* (Cambridge: Cambridge University Press, 1997).

Marx, Karl, and Frederick Engels, *Manifesto of the Communist Party* (Moscow: Progress Publishers, 1952).

Mathewson, Rufus W., *The Positive Hero in Russian Literature* (New York: Columbia University Press, 1958; revised edn, Stanford University Press, 1975).

Mayakovsky, Vladimir, *Polnoe sobranie sochinenii*, 13 vols (Gosudarstvennoe izdatel'stvo khudozhestvennoi literatury, 1955–61). http://az.lib.ru/m/majakowskij_w_w/text_0530.shtml.

Mayakovsky, Vladimir, *My Discovery of America*, trans. Neil Cornwell (London: Hesperus, Modern Voices series, 2005).

Mirsky, D. S., *A History of Russian Literature*, ed. and abridged Francis J. Whitfield (London: Routledge and Kegan Paul, 1968).

Monbiot, George. 'How Ayn Rand Became the New Right's Version of Marx', *The Guardian*, 5 March 2012. https://www.theguardian.com/commentisfree/2012/mar/05/new-right-ayn-rand-marx.

Monbiot, George, 'There Is a Civil War in Capitalism, and We're the Collateral Damage', *The Guardian*, Wednesday, 25 November 2020, *Journal*, 1–2.

Moser, Charles A., *Antinihilism in the Russian Novel of the 1860's* (The Hague: Mouton, 1964).

Moser, Charles A., *Esthetics as Nightmare: Russian Literary Theory, 1855–1870* (Princeton: Princeton University Press, 1989).

Nathans, Benjamin, *Beyond the Pale: The Jewish Encounter with Late Imperial Russia* (Berkeley, Los Angeles and London: University of California Press, 2002).

Offord, Derek, 'Dostoyevsky and Chernyshevsky', *The Slavonic and East European Review* 57, no. 4 (October 1979), 509–30.

Offord, Derek, 'Literature and Ideas in Russia after the Crimean War: The "Plebeian" Writers', in *Ideology in Russian Literature*, ed. Richard Freeborn and Jane Grayson (Basingstoke and London: Macmillan, 1990), 47–78.

Offord, Derek, 'Worshipping the Golden Calf: The Intelligentsia's Conception of the Bourgeois World in the Age of Nicholas', in *Turgenev and Russian*

Culture: Essays to Honour Richard Peace, ed. Joe Andrew, Derek Offord and Robert Reid (Amsterdam and New York: Rodopi, 2008), 237–57.

Offord, Derek, 'Ayn Rand's *Fountainhead* and Its Russian Antecedents', *Modern Language Review* 115, no. 4 (October 2020), 763–90.

Packer, George, 'How America Fractured into Four Parts', *The Atlantic*, July/ August 2021. George Packer: The Four Americas – The Atlantic.

Paperno, Irina, *Chernyshevsky and the Age of Realism: A Study in the Semiotics of Behavior* (Stanford: Stanford University Press, 1988).

Peace, Richard, 'Nihilism', in *A History of Russian Thought*, ed. William Leatherbarrow and Derek Offord (Cambridge: Cambridge University Press, 2010), 116–40.

Pisarev, D. I., *Sochineniia*, 4 vols (Moscow: Gosudarstvennoe izdatel'stvo khudozhestvennoi literatury, 1955–6).

Rand, Ayn, *The Virtue of Selfishness: A New Concept of Egoism* (New York: New American Library, 1964).

Rand, Ayn, *Capitalism: The Unknown Ideal* (New York: A Signet Book, 1967).

Rand, Ayn, *The Romantic Manifesto: A Philosophy of Literature*, 2nd revised edn (New York: Signet, 1975).

Rand, Ayn, *Journals of Ayn Rand*, ed. David Harriman, with a foreword by Leonard Peikoff (New York: Plume, 1999).

Rand, Ayn, *The Fountainhead* (London: Penguin Random House UK, 2007).

Rand, Ayn, *Atlas Shrugged* (London: Penguin Books, 2007).

Rand, Ayn, *We the Living*, with an introduction by Leonard Peikoff (London: Penguin, 2009).

Rand, Ayn, *Anthem* (2016). http://klausnordby.com/anthem/Anthem.pdf.

Rosenthal, Bernice Glatzer (ed.), *Nietzsche in Russia* (Princeton: Princeton University Press, 1986).

Saint-Andre, Peter, 'Zamyatin and Rand', *Journal of Ayn Rand Studies* 4, no. 2 (2003), 285–304.

Scanlan, James P., *Dostoevsky the Thinker* (Ithaca and London: Cornell University Press, 2002).

Sciabarra, Chris Matthew, *Ayn Rand: The Russian Radical* (University Park: Pennsylvania University Press, 1995); 2nd augmented edn 2013 (digital).

Sylvester, Rachel, 'Both Sides Now: Inside the Rise of Sajid Javid', *Prospect*, 27 January 2019. https://www.prospectmagazine.co.uk/politics/both-sides-now-inside-the-rise-of-sajid-javid.

Turgenev, I. S., *Polnoe sobranie sochinenii i pisem*, 28 vols (Moscow and Leningrad: Izdatel'stvo Akademii nauk SSSR, 1961–8).

Weiner, Adam, *How Bad Writing Destroyed the World: Ayn Rand and the Literary Origins of the Financial Crisis* (New York, etc.: Bloomsbury Academic, 2016).

INDEX

Acmeism 17

Aesopian language 65

aestheticism 17, 20

aesthetics or aesthetic questions 19, 29, 30, 37, 40, 53, 61, 97, 102

Aksakov, Konstantin Sergeevich (1817–60) 88

Alexander I (1777–1825; reigned 1801–25) 27

Alexander II (1818–81; reigned 1855–81) 13, 27, 28, 38, 71

Alexander III (1845–94; reigned 1881–94) 12, 27, 39

Algarotti, Francesco (1712–64) 9

altruism 11, 33, 99 *See also under* characters in Rand's novels *and* Rand

American Constitution 78, 85, 95

American frontiersman 95

anarchism 75

Anthem See under Rand

anti-communism (of Rand) 44

anti-Semitism (in pre-revolutionary Russia) 12–16

apocalypse or apocalyptic novel 19, 22, 83, 101

ARI *See* Ayn Rand Institute

aristocracy of money 100

Aristotle (384–22 BC) 21, 70, 81

Asia 90, 93, 101

Atlantis (utopian community in *Atlas Shrugged*) 76–84 *See also* Galt's Gulch

Atlas Shrugged See under Rand

Ayn Rand Institute (ARI) 2, 31

bad writing *See plokhopis'*

Balzac, Honoré de (1799–1850) 2, 56

Beethoven, Ludwig van (1770–1827) 19

Belinsky, Vissarion Grigor'evich (1811–48) 35, 88

Belyi, Andrei (pseudonym of Boris Nikolaevich Bugaev, 1880–1934) 17

Benois, Aleksandr Nikolaevich (1870–1960) 17

Berdiaev, Nikolai Aleksandrovich (1874–1948) 18, 19

Black Hundreds (anti-Semitic mobs) 13

Blanc, Louis (1811–82) 88

Blok, Aleksandr Aleksandrovich (1880–1921) 17

'The Twelve' 19

Bloody Sunday (9 January 1905) 9

Blumenthal, Nathan (1930–2014; he renamed himself Nathaniel Branden after meeting Rand) 5, 12, 32

Bolsheviks 10, 16, 17, 56–7, 86, 90

dictatorship 11

ideology 24

methods 53, 78

politburo 14

Brahms, Johannes (1833–97) 19

Branden, Barbara, *née* Weidman (1929–2013) 11, 12, 15, 20, 31, 37, 78, 81, 82, 92

Branden, Nathaniel *See* Blumenthal

Index

Briusov, Valerii Iakovlevich
        (1873–1924) 17
Bulgakov, Sergei Nikolaevich
        (1871–1944) 18
Bund (Jewish labour organization) 13
Bunin, Ivan Alekseevich
        (1870–1953) 17
Burns, Jennifer 3

Cabet, Étienne (1788–1856) 88
Capitalist Realism 59
categories of human being 29, 65–6,
        86 *See also* extraordinary
        humans *and* ordinary
        humans
Catherine II (Catherine the Great,
        1729–96; reigned 1762–96)
        12
Chaadaev, Petr Iakovlevich
        (1794–1856) 89
    first 'Philosophical Letter' 89
Chait, Jonathan 3
characters in Rand's novels
    Andrei Taganov 41, 67, 78
    Balph Eubank 81
    Dagny Taggart
        on altruism 62–3
        attitude to destroyers 53–4
        conception of heroes as
            martyrs 55
        development of revolutionary
            consciousness in 57, 68
        love of mathematics and sci-
            ences 31
        overwhelmed by Galt 69
        as positive heroine 34
        sexual relationships with
            Randian heroes 49
        status as a woman 81
        violence approved by 79
    Dominique Francon 79
    Eddie Willers 34, 53, 66

Ellis Wyatt 47, 95–6
Ellsworth Toohey
    as apparent altruist 62
    denial of free will 74
    on determinism 72
    on Germany and Russia 93
    on individualism 62
    as power-seeker 42–3, 62
    as Randian villain 33, 42
    on self-sacrifice 62
Equality 7-2521 41–2, 69
Floyd Ferris 44, 72, 73
Francisco d'Anconia
    on altruism 63
    on America 94, 95
    on categories of human be-
        ing 66
    on extraordinary humans
        66, 69
    on money 35–6
    on the moral crisis facing the
        world 34, 63
    as Randian hero 34, 57,
        68
    on second-rate humans 67
    on tax collectors 86
    on women 81
Fred Kinnan 46
Gail Wynand 68
Hank Rearden
    commercial motivation of
        45, 85
    development of revolution-
        ary consciousness in 57
    on intellectuals 46
    as Randian hero 34, 35, 68
    as superior human 66
    violence threatened by 96
    see also Rearden Metal
Howard Roark
    on America 43, 94
    court-room oration of 2, 62

as extraordinary or ideal
    man 33–4, 68, 69
lack of family ties 82
as Rand's mouthpiece 62
as rapist 79
on reason 73
as role model for Donald
    Trump 1
on second-rate humans 67
on taxation 45, 85
uncompromising nature of 85
violence used by 79
Hugh Akston 32, 67
James Taggart 34, 45, 64, 67
John Galt
    on altruism 63–4, 80
    on America 80, 95, 96
    on Aristotle 70
    on Asia 93
    broadcast to the nation by 2,
        55, 63, 70, 78, 80, 95
    on dualism 70
    on egoism 63–4
    on Europe 93
    as extraordinary or ideal
        man 33, 49, 69
    generator invented by 50, 63
    on humans as traders 77
    individualism and capitalism
        restored by 54
    lack of family ties 82
    on laws as unnecessary in
        utopia 75–6
    as positive hero 50–1
    on pride 64
    on reason and man's reason-
        ing capacity 73
    as revolutionary striker or
        destroyer 51, 53–4, 58
    on the role of government 78
    on self-sacrifice 35
    as source of revolutionary

    consciousness 54, 68
    on taxation 85–6
    uncompromising nature of
        33, 85
    on volition 74
Kay Ludlow 81
Kira Argounova 20, 31, 41, 67, 78
Leo Kovalensky 21, 41, 92
Lillian Rearden 96
Midas Mulligan 52, 76
Narragansett 76, 78, 85
Nathaniel Taggart 79, 95
Peter Keating 33, 67
Pritchett 72, 73
Ragnar Danneskjöld
    as defender of the rich 35, 55
    on Europe 93
    piracy of 2–3, 53
    as Randian hero 2, 34, 57
    on Robin Hood 86
    terrorist tactics used by 53
    on women 81
Robert Stadler 32, 34, 75
charity 101 *See also* philanthropy
Chekhov, Anton Pavlovich (1860–
    1904) 16, 21
Chernyshevsky, Nikolai Gavrilovich
    (1828–89)
    'Aesthetic Relationship of Art to
        Reality' 37
    on aesthetics 38, 56
    against bourgeois ethic 35
    on democracy 84
    determinism of 72
    on extraordinary humans 65–6,
        68
    on free will 73–4
    Kirsanov 39, 48, 50
    Lopukhov, 39, 48, 50, 89
    monism of 70
    Rakhmetov 39, 50–1, 65, 73
    rational egoism of 39, 61–3, 76

Vera Pavlovna Rozal'skaia 48, 49, 50
What Is to Be Done? 24, 37, 39, 40, 48–51, 61, 65
children (absence of in Rand's world) 82–3
Cicero, Marcus Tullius (106–43 BC) 42
Civil War *See* Russian Civil War
clash of civilizations 7, 87, 90
Cold War 96
Collective (Rand's coterie) 1, 12
collectivism *See under* Rand
communism 8, 44 *See also* anti-communism
Communist Party (of the Soviet Union) 44, 56
communist society 58
communists (in the United States) 40, 44, 96–7
compromise 25, 32–3, 55–6, 85
Constructivism 18
Contemporary, The 28, 38
cooperation 11, 45, 75
cooperative associations 45, 48, 58, 76
Copernicus (1473–1543) 42
Crystal Palace (housing the Great Exhibition of 1851 in London) 49
Cubism 18

Danilevsky, Nikolai Iakovlevich (1822–85)
Russia and Europe 88
DeMille, Cecil B. (1881–1959) 5
Depression *See* Great Depression
deregulation (of economy) 7 *See also* unregulated capitalism
determinism 22, 33, 71–2
Diaghilev, Sergei Pavlovich (1872–1929) 17, 18

Dickens, Charles (1812–70) 2, 56
Dobroliubov, Nikolai Aleksandrovich (1836–61) 38, 40, 56
Dostoevsky, Fedor Mikhailovich (1821–81)
Alesha Karamazov 42, 89, 96
on America 89
anti-Semitism of 12
The Brothers Karamazov 37, 39, 42, 77
Crime and Punishment 22, 37, 39, 65–6, 101–2
on democracy 84
The Devils 19, 37, 42, 47, 75, 89
The Diary of a Writer 12
engagement in debates of 1860s 23–4
on extraordinary humans and their rights (according to Raskol'nikov) 65–6, 68, 79, 101
The Idiot 19
influence of in Russian Silver Age 19, 20
Ivan Karamazov 39, 42, 69, 75, 89
Kirillov 89
'Legend of the Grand Inquisitor' (in *The Brothers Karamazov*) 42, 75
on money or bourgeois ethic 35, 101
Notes from Underground 73
Rand's debt to 101–2
Raskol'nikov 39, 66, 68, 79, 101
on reason or reasoning capacity 73
on self-sacrifice 34, 61, 63
Shatov 89
Shigalev 42, 75
as thinker as well as novelist 29
on totalitarianism or despotism 42, 75

underground man 73, 77
on the West as a graveyard 89
Winter Notes on Summer Impressions 61
Zosima 77
see also under Rand
dualism (philosophical explanation of world as containing both matter and spirit) 70–1, 100
Duggan, Lisa 4
dystopia or dystopian states 49, 55, 65, 76, 93, 96 *See also* novel, dystopian; Rand, *Anthem*; Zamiatin, *We*

egoism *See under* characters in Rand's novels *and* Rand *See also* rational egoism *under* Chernyshevsky *and* Rand
emancipation of women 48, 81–2
Engels, Friedrich (1820–95) 24, 76 *See also under* Marx
Europe
compared to America by Mayakovsky 90–1
dystopian state of, according to Rand 43, 46
as a graveyard 89
as the old world 47, 48, 88
relation to Russia 87–90
see also under Rand
extraordinary humans 33, 49, 65–70, 75, 79, 84–5 *See also under* Chernyshevsky *and* Dostoevsky *and* characters in Rand's novels

families *See* Rand, on the family
February Revolution (of 1917) 10

Feuerbach, Ludwig Andreas (1804–72) 71
Filosofov, Dmitrii Vladimirovich (1872–1940) 18
First World War (1914–18) 13, 18
Fountainhead See under Rand
Fourier, François-Marie-Charles (1772–1837) 88
free-market economics *See* capitalism *and* central economic planning *under* Rand
free will 7, 33, 73–4
Furmanov, Dmitrii Andreevich (1891–1926) *Chapaev* 57
Futurism 17, 18, 90

Galileo (1564–1642) 68
Galt's Gulch (utopian community in *Atlas Shrugged*) 46, 50, 52, 75 *See also* Atlantis
Gippius, Zinaida Nikolaevna (1869–1945) 18
Gladkov, Fedor Vasil'evich (1883–1958) 58
Gogol', Nikolai Vasil'evich (1809–52) 28
Goncharov, Ivan Aleksandrovich (1812–81) 28
Goncharova, Natal'ia Sergeevna (1881–1962) 18
Gorky, Maksim (pseudonym of Aleksei Maksimovich Peshkov, 1868–1936) 17, 56, 89
The Mother 58
graveyard (as image of Europe in Russian thought) 89, 94
Great Depression 4
Greenspan, Alan 1

Index

Gumilev, Nikolai Stepanovich
(1886–1921) 17

Hannan, Daniel 1
Harriman, David 22–3
Heller, Anne C. 8
Herzen, Alexander (Aleksandr
      Ivanovich Gertsen, 1812–70)
   on America 89
   The Bell 27
   on democracy 84
   From the Other Shore 88
   Letters from France and Italy
      88
   on Russia and Europe 88–9
   as thinker as well as novelist 35
   Who Is to Blame? 43
Hitler, Adolf (1889–1945) 93
Hollywood 5, 95
House Un-American Activities
      Committee (HUAC), Rand's
      testimony to 96–7
Hugo, Victor-Marie (1802–85) 10
humility 64, 101
Huxley, Aldous (1894–1963)
   Brave New World 42

ideinost' (ideological content) 59
   See also Socialist Realist
      literature
Ignat'ev, Nikolai Pavlovich (1832–
      1908) 13
Impressionists 19
individualism *See under* characters
      in Rand's novels *and* Rand
intelligentsia
   angry or accusatory tone of 6, 32
   composition of 28
   duty felt by 29, 34–5
   polarized thinking of 6
   positivistic mindset of 31
   questions addressed by 6, 29–30,
      87, 97

Rand's affinities with or debt
      to 6, 24–5, 30–2, 36–7, 49,
      102
   relation to literary community
      29
   social and political commitment
      of 17, 28–9
   unmercenariness of 35
   way of thinking and writing of
      32–6
   world-outlook of 30–1
   see also under Rand
Ivanov, Viacheslav Ivanovich
      (1866–1949) 17

Javid, Sajid 1–2
Jews, position of in pre-
      revolutionary Russia 12–16

Kamenev, Lev (Lev Borisovich
      Rozenfel'd, 1883–1936) 14
Kandinsky Vasilii Vasil'evich
      (1866–1944) 18
Kepler, Johannes (1571–1630) 66
Kerensky, Aleksandr Fedorovich
      (1881–1970) 10
Keynes, John Maynard (1883–1946)
      5
Khlebnikov, Velimir (Viktor
      Vladimirovich Khlebnikov,
      1885–1922) 17
Khomiakov, Aleksei Stepanovich
      (1804–60) 88
Kireevsky, Ivan Vasil'evich
      (1806–56) 88
Kolchak, Aleksandr Vasil'evich
      (1874–1920) 58
Korolenko, Vladimir Galaktionovich
      (1853–1921) 89
Kravchinsky, Sergei Mikhailovich
      (pen name Stepniak,
      1851–95)
   Andrei Kozhukhov 48

Landmarks 18
Larionov, Mikhail Fedorovich
    (1881–1964) 18
Lavrov, Petr Lavrovich (1823–1900)
    Historical Letters 35
Lenin (Vladimir Il'ich Ul'ianov,
    1870–1924) 39, 51, 53, 70, 90
    What Is to Be Done? 39
Leningrad 90 *See also* Petrograd; St
    Petersburg
Leskov, Nikolai Semenovich
    (1831–95)
    No Way Out 47
Lossky, Nikolai Onufrievich
    (1870–1965) 20
Lycurgus 66

McCarthy, Joseph Raymond
    (1908–57) 96
McCarthyism 59
Malevich, Kasimir Severinovich
    (1879–1935) 18
Martov (Iulii Osipovich
    Tsederbaum, 1873–1923) 13
martyrdom
    of Rand heroes 55–6, 68
    of Socialist Realist heroes 57–8
Marx, Karl (1818–83) 24, 54–5
    (with Engels) *Manifesto of the
    Communist Party* 54–5
Marxian characterization of
    religion 71
Marxian utopia 76
Marxism 18, 54–5, 56
Marxism-Leninism 56, 57
materialism (desire for financial
    success) 85
materialism (philosophical
    doctrine) 61
Mayakovsky, Vladimir
    Vladimirovich (1893–1930)
    17, 20, 89
    My Discovery of America 90–1

Mendeleev, Dmitrii Ivanovich
    (1834–1907) 12
Merezhkovsky, Dmitrii Sergeevich
    (1865–1941) 18, 19
Mohammed (*c.* 570–632) 66
Monbiot, George 86
monism 71
mysticism *See under* Rand

Nabokov, Vladimir Vladimirovich
    (1899–1977) 10
Nabokova, Ol'ga Vladimirovna
    (1903–78) 10
Napoleon Bonaparte (1769–1821) 66
Native-Soil Conservatives 88
New Deal (of Franklin D.
    Roosevelt) 4
New Jerusalem 66, 80, 94
new people 38, 65 *See also*
    extraordinary humans *and*
    positive hero
New Times 12
New Way 18
new world (i.e. America or Russia or
    new way of living) 62, 88–91
Newton, Isaac (1643–1727) 66
Nicholas I (1796–1855; reigned
    1825–55) 27, 43
Nicholas II (1868–1918; reigned
    1894–1917) 12
Nietzsche, Friedrich Wilhelm
    (1844–1900) 21, 78, 101
    Thus Spoke Zarathustra 21
    Übermensch, conception of 21, 69
nihilists 24, 32, 53, 54
Notes of the Fatherland 28
novel (as a genre)
    anti-nihilist 47
    dystopian 41–7
    of ideas 36–40, 42, 95
    revolutionary 48–56
    see also Socialist Realist
    literature

O'Connor, Frank (1897–1979; Rand's husband from 1929) 5, 12, 19, 32, 44

Objectivism (Rand's philosophy) 31

October Revolution (1917) 10, 16, 17, 19, 24

Official Nationalists 88

old world (i.e. Western Europe or Rand's dystopian world) 19, 48, 78, 90, 94

oppositions (in the thought of Rand and the Russian intelligentsia) 33, 88, 92–3, 102

ordinary humans 33, 65–8, 83, 84

Orwell, George (Eric Blair, 1903–50)
  1984 42
  Animal Farm 42

Ostrovsky, Nikolai Alekseevich (1904–36)
  How Steel Was Tempered 57

Owen, Robert (1771–1858) 88

pacifism *See* Rand, non-aggression or non-initiation principle

Pale of Settlement (of Jews in Imperial Russia) 12–15

Pan-Slavists 88

partiinost' (party-mindedness) 56 *See also* Socialist Realist literature

Pasteur, Louis (1822–95) 68

Peikoff, Leonard, 22, 23

People's Will (Russian revolutionary party) 13

Peter the Great (1672–1725; sole ruler of Russia 1696–1725) 9, 87

Petrograd 9, 10, 16, 37, 90, 93 *See also* St Petersburg

Petrograd University (Rand's alma mater) 10, 20, 38, 92

philanthropy 45, 99 *See also* charity

Pisarev, Dmitrii (1840–68) 24, 38, 40, 53, 56
  'Bazarov' 65
  on categories of human being 65–6
  as a destroyer 53
  'Destruction of Aesthetics' 38

Pisemsky, Aleksei (1821–81)
  Troubled Seas 47

Plato (*c.* 427–328 BC) 38, 40

plokhopis' (bad writing) 39–40

Pogodin, Mikhail Petrovich (1800–76) 88

pogroms 13, 14

polarized thinking *See under* intelligentsia *See also* oppositions

Pompeo, Mike 1

popovichi (sons of clergymen) 28

Populists (nineteenth-century Russian revolutionaries) 35, 89

populists (twenty-first-century politicians claiming to represent interests of ordinary people) 46, 97

positive hero (as literary type) 38–40, 50–8, 62, 68, 74 *See also* extraordinary humans; new people; Socialist Realist literature

pride 64, 101

Primitivism 18

production novel 58–9 *See also* Socialist Realist literature

Prometheus 69

publitsistika (Russian topical journalism) 28

Pushkin, Alexander Sergeevich (1799–1837) 20, 27

Puzder, Andrew 1

Rachmaninov, Sergei Vasil'evich (1873–1943) 18, 19
rape *See under* Rand
Rand, Ayn
  on America's glorious past 43, 94–6
  American context of her novels 4–5
  Americanism, conception of 7, 97
  Anthem 41–2, 43, 69
  arrival in United States 5
  artistic standard of her novels 2–3
  Atlas Shrugged
    affinities with the Socialist Realist novel 56–9
    as an apocalyptic novel 101
    as a Cold-War novel 96
    compared to the Tolstoyan novel 82
    as a critique of altruism and defence of egoism 62–4
    as a dystopian novel 43–7
    messianism in 34, 94
    opposition between Randian heroes and their enemies in 33–4
    pre-eminence in Rand's œuvre 8
    resemblance to Cherny-shevsky's *What Is to Be Done?* 48–51
    as a revolutionary novel 51–6
    as a study of extraordinary and ordinary humans 66–70
    as a utopian novel 75–9
  capitalism, defence or praise of 3, 6, 31, 45, 48, 54, 56, 77
  on central economic planning 44, 56–7
  childhood experience of 10–11
  on collectivism or collective endeavour or ownership 5, 47, 58, 62, 76, 82
  on democracy 7, 22, 25, 85, 86
  on determinism 71–2
  on Dostoevsky 21–2, 23–4 (*see also* Dostoevsky, Rand's debt to)
  dystopia, conception of 49–50, 55
  on economic distribution 3, 7, 85–6, 91
  empathy, lack of 3, 64
  on ends and means 53, 54, 70
  Europe, negative view of 92–4, 97
  extrinsic and intrinsic worth of her writings 3–4
  on the family as a unit 15–16, 25, 48, 49, 82
  The Fountainhead
    as a critique of altruism 62
    as a dystopian novel 43
    as an overture to *Atlas Shrugged* 8
    as a study of superior and second-rate humans 67–9
  on free will 73–4
  graveyard as image of Europe in writings of 94
  on 'hitchhikers' 67
  on humility 64, 101
  individualism, defence of 6, 54, 56, 96 (*see also* 'Manifesto of Individualism' *below*)
  intellectual and literary influences on 20–4
  on intelligentsia or intellectuals 46–7, 67, 71–2
  inversion of normal valuations of altruism and egoism 7, 62–4
  Jewish background of 12–16

Index

Journals of Ayn Rand 22
on 'looters' 55, 67
'Manifesto of Individualism'
    44, 54
on mysticism, mystics or the
    'mystic(al)' 21, 92–6
New York, admiration for
    49–50, 52
nihilistic traits of 32
non-aggression or non-
    initiation principle 78–9
parents of 15
personality of 11–12
rape, treatment of 79
rational egoism of 51, 77, 82, 86
on reason or power of reasoning
    31, 35, 49, 72–6, 83–5, 99
relations with mother 11, 64
sales of novels 2
schooling and university 10
on 'second-handers' 67, 80
on 'second-raters' 67, 80, 85
on skyscrapers 20, 49–50, 55
on social democracy 8, 45
socialism, antipathy to 8, 11,
    16, 97
sociopathic nature of her heroes
    64
subversion of Marxist concepts
    and vocabulary 54–5
on totalitarianism 12, 44,
    45, 93, 97 (*see also under*
    Dostoevsky)
utopia, conception of 7, 36, 45,
    49, 63, 66, 75–83, 84, 85, 94
    (*see also* Atlantis *and* Galt's
    Gulch)
on victimhood of heroes of 55,
    76, 78
We the Living 9, 20, 21, 41, 43,
    46, 67, 78
see also characters in Rand's
    novels

rational egoism *See under*
    Chernyshevsky *and* Rand
Rayonism 18
raznochintsy (non-noble
    members of Russian
    intelligentsia) 28
Reaganites 1
Rearden Metal 34, 45, 50, 53, 59
reason *See under* Dostoevsky *and*
    Rand *and under* characters
    in Rand's novels
Red Decade (in United States) 4
Religious-Philosophical Meetings
    18
renaissance
    as envisaged by Rand 34
    in Russian Silver Age 16–20
Revelation, Book of 80
Revolution of 1905 9, 13, 29
revolutionary situation (as defined
    by Lenin) 51
Rimsky-Korsakov, Nikolai
    Andreevich (1844–1908) 18
Roosevelt, Franklin Delano
    (1882–1945) 4, 44
Rosenbaum, Alisa Zinov'evna *See*
    Rand
Rozanov, Vasilii Vasil'evich
    (1856–1919) 19
Russian Civil War (1918–22) 10,
    56–8
Russian Social-Democratic Labour
    Party (RSDLP) 13–14
Russian Socialism (of Herzen)
    89
Russian socialists 24, 35, 48
Ryan, Paul 1

St Petersburg 9, 14–15, 16, 19, 24,
    37, 92 *See also* Petrograd
Scriabin, Aleksandr Nikolaevich
    (1872–1915) 18
Second World War (1939–45) 4

self-sacrifice 29, 34–5 *See also under* characters in Rand's novels *and* Dostoevsky
sexual mores 25, 32
sexual violence 3, 79
Shakespeare, William (1564–1616) 42
Shestov, Lev Isaakovich (1866–1938) 19
Silicon Valley 1
Silver Age (of Russian culture) 6, 16–20, 21, 34
skyscrapers *See under* Rand
Slavophiles 88, 92
Sleptsov, Vasilii Alekseevich (1836–78)
    Hard Times 48
smoking 32, 57
Snitkina, Anna Grigor'evna (1846–1918) 10
socialism *See* Russian Socialism; Russian socialists; Socialist Realist literature *See also under* Rand
Socialist Realist literature 56–9, 74, 95 *See also ideinost'*; *partiinost'*; positive hero; production novel; *soznatel'nost'*
Socrates (469–399 BC) 68
Sologub (pen name of Fedor Kuz'mich Teternikov, 1863–1927)
    Little Demon 17
Solon (*c.* 630–*c.* 570 BC) 66
Solzhenitsyn, Aleksandr Isaevich (1918–2008) 21
soznatel'nost' (philosophical and political consciousness) 57
    See also Socialist Realist literature
Stalin, Joseph (Iosif Vissarionovich Dzhugashvili, 1879–1953) 95

Stoiunina, Mariia Nikolaevna (1846–1940) 10
strike (as revolutionary tactic) 51
Suprematism 18
Suvorin, Aleksei Sergeevich (1834–1912) 12
Symbolism 17

taxation 4, 7, 8, 45, 79, 85–6, 100
    See also under characters in Rand's novels
Tea Party 1
Tillerson, Rex 1
Titans 69, 81
Tocqueville, Alexis Charles-Henri Clérel de (1805–59)
    Democracy in America 89
Tolstoy, Lev Nikolaevich (1828–1910) 16, 21, 28, 56, 83
    as anarchist 75
    Resurrection 37
    as thinker as well as novelist 29
    War and Peace 82
    What Is Art? 37
train crash (in Colorado tunnel, in *Atlas Shrugged*) 46–7, 79
Trotsky, Leon (Lev Davidovich Bronshtein, 1879–1940) 14
Trotskyites 58
Trump, Donald 1
Turgenev, Ivan Sergeevich (1818–83) 16, 20, 28, 38
    Bazarov 24, 39, 53
    Fathers and Children 24, 37, 53, 65
    Insarov 39
    On the Eve 39

Übermensch See under Nietzsche
Ul'ianov, Aleksandr Il'ich (elder brother of Lenin; 1866–87) 39
Union of the Russian People 13

unregulated capitalism or
    unregulated free market
    6, 8, 45, 77, 100 *See also*
    deregulation
utilitarian literary criticism 38
utilitarianism 61, 63
utopia *See under* Rand *See also*
    Atlantis *and* Galt's Gulch
utopian socialists (Fourier *et al.*)
    24, 88

violence *See under* characters
    in Rand's novels *See also*
    Rand, non-aggression or
    non-initiation principle *and*
    sexual violence
volition 72, 73–4, 84 *See also* free
    will *and* free will *under*
    Chernyshevsky *and* Rand

Wall Street Crash (1929) 4
warlord capitalism 86

We the Living See under Rand
Weiner, Adam 39
Wells, H. G. (Herbert George Wells,
    1866–1946)
    War of the Worlds 91
West, in Russian thought 87–90
Westernizers 88, 92, 94
Willkie, Wendell Lewis
    (1892–1944) 44
women *See* emancipation of
    women *and under* characters
    in Rand's novels
World of Art 17
World's Fair (1937, in Paris) 82

Zamiatin, Evgenii Ivanovich
    (1884–1937)
    We 43, 83
Zinov'iev, Grigorii Evseevich
    (Hirsch Apfelbaum,
    1883–1936) 14
Zola, Émile (1840–1902) 56